THE REASONINGS

THE RISALE-I NUR COLLECTION

THE REASONINGS

A Key to Understanding the Qur'an's Eloquence

BEDİÜZZAMAN SAİD NURSİ

Translated by Hüseyin Akarsu

TUGHRA
BOOKS
New Jersey

Copyright © 2022 by Tughra Books

25 24 23 22   2 3 4 5

Published by Tughra Books

335 Clifton Ave

Clifton, NJ 07011

www.tughrabooks.com

Library of Congress Cataloging-in-Publication Data

Nursi, Said, 1873-1960.
  [Risale-i nur. English. Selections]
  The reasonings : a key to understanding the Qur'an's eloquence / Bediuzzaman Said Nursi.
      p. cm.
  Includes index.
  ISBN 978-1-59784-129-0 (hardcover)
  1. Koran--Criticism, interpretation, etc. 2. Koran--Appreciation. 3. Koran--Language, style. 4. Nurculuk--Doctrines. I. Title.
  BP252.N85213 2008
  297.8'3--dc22

                                                                2008021228

Table of Contents

THE FIRST PART
THE ELEMENT OF TRUTH

THE SECOND PART
THE ESSENCE OF ELOQUENCE

THE THIRD PART
THE ELEMENT OF BELIEF

Bediüzzaman and The Reasonings

The end of the nineteenth and the beginning of the twentieth centuries constitute a crucial era from the viewpoint of world history, particularly as far as the Islamic world is concerned. The thinkers—or the apparently thinking minds—of this period in the Islamic world, whose prominence in terms of material power through almost eleven centuries had long been failing, began searching for the causes of, and remedies for, this calamity. They proposed several approaches to pinpoint and treat the problem, yielding attitudes that paved the way for the birth of many currents of thought.

Of these emerging currents, the overall picture presented by what we can call *blind* Westernization was one of trying to coerce the East, in the words of Cemil Meriç,[1] to wear the "straitjacket" of the West without considering the historical and sociological conditions of the East. This trend or current advocated abandonment of the spirit of Islam's thirteen-century-long history. Some Muslims, presuming to speak as scholars, did not hesitate to insist that new currents of thought should be supported and Islam be reformed according to them. On the other hand, other Muslim intellectuals, located somewhere in the middle (or on the periphery) of the two factions just mentioned and who were seemingly more reflective of indigenous

---

1 Cemil Meriç (1916–1987) was one of the well-known thinkers and prolific writers of twentieth-century Turkey. He became known particularly for his analyses of modern Western civilization. Among his books *Umrandan Uygarlığa* ("From 'Umran' to Civilization"), *Bu Ülke* ("This Country"), *Kültürden İrfana* ("From Culture to Spiritual Knowledge"), *Işık Doğudan Gelir* ("Light Comes from the East"), and *Yeni Bir Dünyanın Eşiğinde* ("On the Threshold of a New World") are the most famous.

viewpoints and positions, yet manifestly under the influence of the "winds" blowing around, attempted to present, imprudently and somewhat apologetically, some so-called "antidotes" though it was, in reality, highly questionable whether they were antidotes. Some among them tried to identify Islam with new currents of thought and ideologies, while others reduced it to a political ideology. Thus, they fell into a mistaken interpretation of religion and history, and there even appeared from among them some who called for abandoning the Sunna.

The years we speak of were also years that witnessed heated discussions within Islam regarding numerous issues, the influence of which is felt even today. Just as the development of rational and experimental sciences in the post-Renaissance sparked off discussions regarding the many truths of Christianity and the Old and New Testaments, this era similarly opened the door to a variety of approaches and multi-faceted discussions concerning Islam, the Qur'an, Islamic history, and Islamic sciences. Certainly, the focal point of these discussions was the issue of "how to present the Qur'an or Islam for the understanding of the period." While some who spoke from within this perspective were under the spell of modern science and technology and thus advocated the reinterpretation of the principles of Islam and the Qur'an according to this criterion despite the obvious risk of subjecting those principles to alteration and distortion, others were overly fervent in proposing projects of socio-political reform, and in the name of the Qur'an and the Sunna, turned their back on the Sunna, and on the expanse of Islamic history. This was the atmosphere in which Bediüzzaman Said Nursi, a scholar of great importance, found himself when he arrived in Istanbul, the capital of the Ottoman state in 1907. He studied the traditional Islamic sciences, having profoundly immersed his heart and mind in the Qur'an and the Sunna, while at the same time he adopted a unique, individual manner of not asking any questions from living traditional circles, in addition to studying natural sciences and following new developments in sciences and technology.

In the face of the "avant-garde-ists," who evidently perceived Islam as a hindrance to development and associated the West's scientific and military advances with its "negative" outlook on religion, Bediüzzaman Said Nursi declared, "I shall prove to the world that the Qur'an is a spiritual sun that cannot be extinguished." It was in such an atmosphere that Said Nursi worked toward the construction of an indestructible fortress around the Qur'an, undeterred by the blasts detonated internally or externally, and thus opted to be a tireless servant in the implementation of the Divine declaration, "*Indeed it is We, We Who send down the Reminder* (i.e. the Qur'an), *and it is indeed We Who are its Guardian*" (al-Hijr, 15:9). As a scholar who had studied almost all the positive or natural sciences of his day, he reflected, to a certain extent, the influence of modern scientific data and philosophy used to corroborate the realities of the Qur'an in his early works, where he addresses others using their own brand of logic. Later on, he asserts, "Only what has been sanctified by the Qur'an may act as corroboration for the Qur'an. Substantiating the Qur'an with whatever is not in accord with it means demoting it to a degree." However, he never despised or ignored any truth wherever it is found, in accordance with the Prophetic Tradition: "Wisdom is like the lost property of believers. Wherever they find it, they have a greater right to take it."[2] He was the embodiment of a distinguished spiritual master and a noble character full of respect for his history and predecessors, attached to tradition but open to new developments, endowed with love of truth, uncompromising in the face of imitation, sober and vigorous in evaluating ideas and situations, and dignified by the highest degree of faith. He carried only the purest of intentions—to earn the good pleasure of God and serve humanity.

According to Nursi, the core of Islam had been, to a certain extent, abandoned during the last few centuries, resulting in an emphasis on the surface of things. The result was that the Qur'an, which contains both verses that are decisive and explicit in meaning and content and allegorical statements, and therefore sometimes uses a symbolic language and literary arts—such as similes, allegories, and metaphors—as it addresses all times and levels of understanding, could not be comprehended sufficiently both by its friend and foe. Thus, some of the finer requirements of Islam were neither understood nor realized owing to misunderstandings and disrespect, as the critical language of symbolism was taken strictly at face value. This was one of the basic reasons that prevented the actualization of Islam which, in turn, culminated in the punishment of the Muslims in this world with both abasement and privation.

---

[2]   al-Tirmidhi, *Sunan*, "'Ilm" 19; Ibn Maja, *Sunan*, "Zuhd" 17.

Simply put, what can save Muslims is Islam's compassion. Therefore, Muslims must apologize and pay homage to their own religion. Subsequently, the true path that exists within Islam must be delineated; the confusion imposed by those who do not sufficiently understand matters must be dispelled; the arguments of those opposed to the religion must be voided and demonstrated to be unworkable; and those aspiring toward this cause must be assisted. In brief, Islam or Islamic perception and practice, although temporarily covered in dust, can and must be restored to its original luster. And Nursi's *Muhakemat* ("The Reasonings") was written specifically with this intention and effort in mind.

So, from which perspective should one approach Islam and the Qur'an? What are the purposes and the objectives set out by the Qur'an, and what method must one utilize to realize these objectives? In addition, what relevance do the methods of the experimental sciences in particular have in this context? Why has science flown from the hands of Muslims? Is the Qur'an itself responsible in any way for this bereavement? What are the reasons behind different opinions concerning certain Qur'anic verses? What are the elements of rhetoric, and what is the rhetorical style of the Qur'an? How should we construe the meaning of an utterance? Where has the door to superstition been left ajar? And what are the principal characteristics of true meaning? What must our approach and principles be in handling the issues? Where are good and evil to be found? What is the wisdom and rationality behind them? Where is Hell? And so on. In his unique style, in addition to giving convincing answers to such and many other questions, Nursi also examines the difference between contingency and the absolute; the formation of discourse as well as its prosodic features, strength, vastness, profundity, and effects; the imperative of rhetoric; the proofs of the existence of God; the substantiation of Prophethood; and the debate revolving around bodily resurrection. Particularly in understanding the Qur'an, *The Reasonings* is indeed a book of "wisdom" and "measures." It is also a wonderful introduction to Nursi's other work, *Isharat al-I'jaz* ("Signs of the Qur'an's Miraculousness"), which is a splendid key to the exegesis of the Qur'an. *The Reasonings* is an indispensable guide for aspirers to knowledge who wish to obtain robust understanding amid the web of decades of dispute, and to unshackle themselves from excess and apathy. Let us take a brief look at some excerpts from *The Reasonings*:

- The Qur'an throughout all of its verses aims mainly to establish and confirm four basic, universal truths: the existence and Oneness of the Maker of the universe; Prophethood; bodily Resurrection; and worship and justice.

- Something theoretical in the past may become evident and established in the present or in the future. It is a self-evident fact that creation has an innate tendency towards perfection, and it is through this that creation is bound to the law of development or gradual perfection.

- One who is much occupied in a subject is usually more insensitive to other subjects and cannot understand these so well.

- Those who search for every truth in corporeality have their intellects in their corporeal senses, when corporeal senses are blind to spiritual things.

- What reliably interprets the Qur'an is primarily the Qur'an itself and the reliably narrated Hadith.

- Not everything mentioned in the exposition of the Qur'an must necessarily be "exposition."

- Common opinion demands a new interpretation of the Qur'an. Each age has characteristics peculiar to itself and therefore has its own needs and demands. Time adds its own interpretation, and new events and developments cause many new meanings to be discovered.

- Fame exaggerates, presenting one as owning what one does not own.

- Attributing to anything or anyone more good than God has attributed to them is not a positive move, nor does it mean that you have done them any good. A single grain of truth is preferable to a bumper harvest of false imaginings. We must be content with defining something or someone with the good God has accorded them in creation and the virtues they have.

- When passing from the hands of knowledge to the hands of ignorance, a metaphorical expression may change into a literal description and open a door to superstition.

- One who cannot discover the kernel becomes occupied with and restricted to the shell. One who does not know the truth deviates to whims and fancies. One who cannot detect or find the straight path goes to extremes. One who does not have a true balance not only deceives others, but is greatly deceived.

Unfortunately, we cannot claim that the *The Reasonings* has been read to the extent it should be nor received the attention it undoubtedly deserves in the country where it was written and published mostly because of the alleged impenetrability of its language and content. Consequently, hoping that there will be many who can understand it in other regions of the world, in due appreciation of it, we have dared to translate it. In the process, if we have fallen into error or have been presumptuous in relation to this masterpiece and its author, we seek the forgiveness of God the Almighty, of the work, and of its writer.

The Publisher

The Prescription for a Morbid Era, a Diseased Unit,
and a Disabled System; or
Showing Islam's Pristine Brilliance; or
Bediüzzaman's Reasonings

Preface

In the Name of God, the All-Merciful, the All-Compassionate.

 debt of deepest reverence and submission is due to the Eternal Sovereign, the All-Wise and All-Merciful, Who has blessed us with the religion of Islam and given us guidance in the form of the pure and peerless Shari'a.[3] This Shari'a is a code of law the truth of which has been confirmed by human intellect and Divine Revelation; it is a corpus of rules so veracious that its roots reach deeply into the soil of truth, producing in human individual and social life branches of perfection which bear the fruit of happiness in this world and the next. The Shari'a has also helped us to attain intellectual and spiritual maturity through the grace of the Qur'an, which in all of its aspects is a Divine miracle.

Through the rules and principles it outlines, the Holy Qur'an expounds the subtle, all-inclusive Divine laws which are operative in the cosmos; it is a Divine Book of creation which the Hand of Destiny has inscribed with the Pen of Wisdom. There is in the Qur'an all that humanity needs for a well-ordered and harmonious life, and all that it needs in order that it may progress.

---

3   Shari'a is the set of the rules and laws established by the Divine Book and the Pr - phetic Traditions (Sunna) to order human religious individual and collective life. (Trans.)

May endless peace and blessings be upon the master of creation, who is the source of pride and honor for this world. The entire universe and all the creatures in it bear witness that Prophet Muhammad is the Messenger of God and that they serve as a means and medium for his miracles, heralding the exalted truths and principles which he brought from the treasury of the Unseen. Each species of creatures, in its own particular tongue, ardently welcomes the honor the Prophet bestowed on the universe with his presence. The Eternal Sovereign causes the needs of the earth and heavens to speak so that each need sings the songs of the Prophet's miracles as if it were a string on the cosmic violin. Thus, his beautiful, thrilling voice will echo in the azure vault of heaven. The heavens congratulate him in the language of his Ascension, as do the angels, and the moon. The earth praises him because of his miracles in the language of its rocks, trees, and animals. The atmosphere gives the glad tidings of his Prophethood with its invisible beings, providing shade for him and protecting him with its clouds. The time preceding the Prophet gives the joyful tidings of the rising of that sun of truth with the other Prophets' confirmation of him, and the predictions of the Scriptures and seers.[4] The blessed age of the Prophet himself proves the Prophethood of Muhammad in the language of the society and state it set in train; that is, by producing the tremendous transformation in the character of the Arabs and giving rise, in so short a time, to a magnificent civilization from a desert life. And the post-Prophetic era thanks him for his guidance with the tongue of wisdom and sciences, heralding his ascension to the highest throne of humanity and Prophethood through the transformations he has engendered in the history of humanity. With its scholars—particularly with the verifying ones among them and those who pay heed to the articulate and eloquent dis-

---

[4]   God allowed the jinn, whom He created with the ability to ascend and penetrate the heaens to listen to the conversations of the angels, to grasp some bits of information from their conversations before the advent of His Last Messenger, Prophet Muhammad, upon him be peace and blessings. So, they ascended the heavens and were able to obtain some information from the angels' conversations, and whispered this to those among the human beings who were in contact with them. Many seers had predicted the coming of Prophet Muhammad, upon him be peace and blessings. However, just prior to his advent, God shut the gates of the heavens to the jinn completely. When they tried to gain entry into the heavens, they found them protected by strong guards who hurled missiles at them. Now if any of the jinn are able to grasp something, they are pursued (and destroyed) by a shooting star dispatched by the angels on guard there. See, the Qur'an, 67: 5; 72: 8–10. (Trans.)

course of the Prophet—humanity bears witness that Muhammad, upon him be peace and blessings, who himself is like a sun which illuminates both itself and others, is a Messenger sent by the Almighty.

A couplet:

> A chain by which all the lions of the world are bound;
> Would it ever be possible for a deceitful fox to break it?

Now, this poor Nursi, whom people have mistakenly and without his consent nicknamed Bediüzzaman—the Peerless of the Age—though he might be called Bid'atüzzaman—the Innovation of the Age—grieves bitterly over the lack of development of this poor nation. With a heart filled with regret, he says: We have abandoned the essence of Islam and concentrated instead on its shell; in doing so, we have deceived ourselves. Having committed mistakes and fallen short of the ethical standards we should have had, we have failed to give Islam its due and the respect it deserves. As a result, it has recoiled from us in disgust, hiding itself in the miasma of whims and suppositions that we have formed around it.

It has the absolute right to do so, for we have been unable to recognize its true worth. We have conflated its fundamentals with spurious accretions from non-Islamic sources; we have commingled its principles of belief with mere stories, confusing people into taking its figurative, metaphorical, and allegorical statements as though they were statements of literal truth. For this reason, Islam has punished us with misery and wretchedness in the world. It is only the mercy of Islam which will save us.

So, O Muslim brothers and sisters! Let us ask forgiveness from Islam and obtain its good pleasure. Together we must stretch the hands of faith to Islam and pay allegiance to it. Together we will hold fast to the unbreakable rope of our religion.

Without any hesitation I can say that what gives me the courage and enthusiasm to confront the thoughts and attitudes of past centuries, and what moves me to exert myself to remove the whims and suppositions that have gained currency over those centuries is this: I believe with the utmost conviction that even though it has been trampled underfoot, the truth will eventually flourish; I also believe that even though they are few in number and weakened by the mercilessness of the present conditions, the supporters of the truth will one day emerge victorious.

I am also convinced that it is only the truth of Islam that will prevail in the future and enjoy absolute authority all around the world. It is only Islam that will be seated on the future throne of truth and knowledge. The signs of this victory have already begun to appear. In the past there were eight obstacles which prevented the light-giving Shari'a from overcoming the despotic rule of fanaticism and blind imitation, and from sweeping aside the deceptively glittering debris of knowledge which held sway over the wasteland of human ignorance. Of these obstacles, which caused the sun of Islam to be eclipsed, four were to be found in the West: blind imitation of the clergy, ignorance, fanaticism, and the hegemony of the Church. Three of these obstacles were dominant in Muslim lands: despotism, disorder in internal affairs, and the kind of hopelessness which leads to apathy. The eighth obstacle, and greatest of all, was to be found both among us and in the West: this was the supposed conflict between certain outer aspects of Islam and a number of established scientific facts. Thanks to the enthusiastic and courageous efforts of scientific knowledge which, out of its love for humanity, has mobilized the truths which emerge from unbiased investigation and judgment, these obstacles have begun to be destroyed.

For sure the greatest obstacle, which causes us to suffer misery in the world and the Westerners to be deprived of happiness in the Hereafter, and which causes the sun of Islam to be eclipsed, is the supposed conflict between some outer aspects of Islam and certain established scientific facts. This is strange, to say the least, for how can something be in conflict with the very phenomenon that has given rise to it? For it is Islam which has shepherded the sciences, and even given birth to many of them. Yet the fallacy of conflict between Islam and science continues to prey on our minds, driving many to hopelessness and serving to close the doors of knowledge and civilization to many of the Muslim people. Those who imagine that Islam is in conflict with science labor under a misapprehension that is fuelled by fear. For example, there are some who think that by believing that the world is round, they will be in contravention of certain Islamic principles—despite the fact that the spherical form of the earth is a clearly established fact confirmed by geography, a discipline which deals with some of the most observable phenomena in the universe.

O friend, my aim in this book is as follows: I seek to show the straight path in Islam, proving false the doubts which its enemies have tried to spread about it, and showing how baseless are the whims and worries of those Muslims who have imprisoned themselves in the faulty understanding of some of the outer aspects of Islam. I also hope to be able to lend a helping hand to those loyal friends of Islam and the truth-seeking scholars who try to lead people to the truth, who strive for development in the Muslim world, and who exert themselves with the hope of victory on the straight path.

In short, my aim is to brush away the dust from Islam and to show it in its pristine brilliance.

If you were to ask why I strive in this way to reveal the truth of matters which have already been clarified and are commonly known, I would say in reply:

It is true that we all live in the same world and in the same era, but intellectually, many of us are still in the Middle Ages. Because of this, there are many obvious truths which are still unclear to them.

Introduction

his book consists of three parts, each of which stands alone. The first part aims to explain the element of truth in Islam, or to show Islam in its pristine brilliance under the headings of *premises* and subheadings of *matters*. The second part discovers the element of *eloquence*. The third part is about the elements of faith and contains answers given to questions asked by some Japanese people.

Taken all together, the parts provide a key to an understanding of the Qur'an from the perspectives of such physical sciences as astronomy and geology, and from social sciences such as anthropology and sociology.

The First Part

The Element of Truth

The First Part
The Element of Truth

The following twelve premises form the ladder we will climb to reach our aim.

The First Premise

It is an established methodological principle (in the Islamic sciences) that when any item of religious knowledge reported to be based on either the Qur'an or the Sunna of the Prophet appears to be in conflict with reason, the judgment of reason—provided that it is genuine—takes priority and, consequently, the item in question is subjected to interpretation.[5]

It is also an established fact that the Qur'an throughout all of its verses aims mainly to establish and confirm four basic, universal truths: the existence and Oneness of the Maker of the universe; Prophethood; bodily Resurrection; and worship and justice. It is the Qur'an alone which is able to give the correct and most persuasive answer to the questions asked of creation by philosophy, namely, "From where and by whose order do you come into existence? Who directs you? Who is your guide and spokesperson? Why

---

5   Genuine reason is that which has been taught and enlightened by the established truths and foundational principles of Islam, and which is implemented by one who possesses accurate knowledge both of God's creational laws and of the laws enshrined in the Divinely-revealed religious code or *Shari'a*. (Trans.)

do you exist and what is your purpose here? What is your final destination?" Except when they are used as evidence to support basic, universal truths, "natural" facts are referred to by the Qur'an only parenthetically, and then simply in order to show how the workings of the cosmos can be understood as leading logically to the All-Majestic Maker through the Divine art on display throughout creation. For clearly there is a magnificent order at work in the universe. This order, which bears decisive witness to the existence of the Maker, to His purpose for the creation of the universe and to His Will, is so apparent throughout the universe that it presents its magnificence and beauty before wisdom and philosophy with the utmost clarity. It is as though each being is a voice praising its Maker's wisdom; indeed, each species indicates this and testifies to it. Since the main purpose of the Qur'an in mentioning the book of the cosmos or in referring to the facts of creation is to prove the existence and Oneness of the Maker, and since one of those facts which is apparent throughout the universe is its order, exactly how the universe was created is not really the issue when we approach the Quran: more important for us is the fact that the universe is a proof of its Creator's existence.

Any cosmic phenomenon that is mentioned in the supreme assemblage of the Qur'an has the following four functions:

Firstly, it proclaims the grandeur of the All-Majestic Maker through the voice of the order of which it is a part, and through being in perfect harmony with all other parts or elements of creation.

Secondly, since it is the subject matter of a particular science, it shows that Islam is the bedrock of all sciences.

Thirdly, since it is representative of a whole species, it clearly exhibits the concord which exists between Islam and the Divine laws at work in the universe. Perceiving this concord allows for Islam to be better understood. For since it is a religion which is, in all of its aspects, in accord with the Divine laws of creation and life, Islam has a distinguished place among the religions, and in particular above those that encourage vacillation between desires and caprices and leave their followers without help; or those which sometimes give light and at other times leave their followers in darkness; or those that are exposed to rapid change and transformation.

Fourthly, since each of the cosmic phenomena is a manifestation of the truth, it serves to arouse, direct, and encourage minds towards the truth.

In short, it serves as a warning to those people who are reluctant to deliberate upon the things on earth and the celestial bodies by which God swears in the Qur'an, the importance of which is stressed therein. Each of the oaths in the Qur'an can be seen as a staff that strikes those who are in the deep sleep of neglect and indifference.

Since this is the truth, there can be no doubt that the guiding Qur'an, which stands at the pinnacle of eloquence and the like of which no person has ever been able to produce, be it even a single verse, has chosen for itself the most appropriate linguistic style and the most concise and direct way of argument. For this reason, and because the vast majority of people do not have expert knowledge of scientific facts, it considers the feelings and sense perceptions of ordinary people in order to convey to them its main themes and guide them to the truth. In other words, it tells us about the perfect order of the universe, which constitutes evidence for the truth of the matters it seeks to establish, in such a style that it does not go unnoticed, even by the average person. Nor is it ambiguous or confusing for them, and it does not leave them in doubt or uncertainty. Had it been otherwise, the evidence would be more indistinct and unclear than the thesis itself; clearly this would not have been in conformity with the guidance, eloquence and inimitability of the Qur'an.

For example, the Qur'an might have declared, "O humankind! Ponder on the earth as it moves through space in orbit around the sun; and the sun which, though moving, is stable on its axis; and the law of general gravity, which ties the celestial bodies one to the other; and the interrelations among the fruits of the tree of creation, which has stretched out its branches through seemingly infinite space! Deliberate upon these facts and consider the grandeur of the Maker of the universe! Also, look with the eye of intellect at a single drop of water with its world of innumerable microorganisms so that you can confirm how powerful the Maker is." Had the Qur'an proceeded in this manner, would the evidence not have been more indistinct and abstruse than the thesis (the purposes it pursues)? Would it not also have been an attempt to explain a truth to the average person by using examples which are unknown or obscure to them? Would it not have seemed like a pedantic attempt to impose on them something which appears irrational and which does not accord with their sense perceptions? The reality of the matter, however, is that the linguistic inimitability of the Qur'an is so elevated and removed from the laborious and the irrational that nothing abstruse or dysfunctional to its pure style can find a place within it.

Another point to mention here is that just as the Qur'an of miraculous expression indicates its basic purposes through the fabric of its verses, it also sheds light on them through the apparent meanings which those verses enshrine.

It is another established principle that truth or falsehood, or confirmation or denial, cannot be gleaned from the apparent meaning of allusive and figurative expressions. It is found in the purpose for which they are uttered or what is meant by them. For example, if we say that a tall person has a sword with a long handle, this is true even if that man does not have a sword, for what we have uttered is a figurative statement designed purely to indicate the height of the man. Moreover, one of the words in this figurative statement has been used metaphorically and gives the statement its meaning. Similarly, some of the verses of the Word of God—the Qur'an— all parts of which are interconnected, point to the gems of truth contained in other verses: they translate the secrets which lie in the hearts of their neighbors.

In short, one who does not consider this fact and is unable to judge the verses as they should be judged stands ridiculed in the face of the truth: he is like a dervish who attempts to make an excuse for his neglect of the daily Prayers by saying, "The Qur'an orders us: 'Do not come forward to (stand in) the Prayer!'", but conveniently omits the end of the verse, "while you are in (any sort of) state of drunkenness until you know what you are saying."

The Second Premise

Something theoretical in the past may become evident and established in the present or in the future. It is a self-evident fact that creation has an innate tendency towards perfection, and it is through this that creation is bound to the law of development or gradual perfection.

Included in creation, human life has a tendency towards progress that arises from this tendency towards perfection. This tendency toward progress becomes possible through opinions and theories being built upon one another over the course of centuries. Opinions and theories develop by means of the results attained—facts; then axioms or principles become established, and means to implement the principles learnt are invented. Established facts and principles impregnate the seeds of sciences that emanate from the "ribs" of creation in the womb of time, where they grow through experience and experimentation.

It is for this reason that many of the matters known to all today were only theoretical or even incomprehensible in the past. We clearly see that many matters of geography, astronomy, physics, chemistry, and other sciences are no longer unknown to the children of today, due to the facts and principles that have been established, the means that have been invented, and the opinions that have gained strength from one another. They were unknown even to Ibn Sina (Avicenna)[6] and thinkers and scientists like him, although such people had a greater capacity and were far better versed in philosophy and sciences than many of their contemporaries. The deficiency lies not in Ibn Sina and his contemporaries, but in the time they lived in; we are all children of our time. Is it not true that if the New World, the discovery of which gave Columbus his fame, had not so far been discovered, any ordinary captain could, at present, make the Old and New Worlds neighbors to each other? A small ship and a compass can substitute for the knowledge of navigation that Columbus had access to, and his daring and resistance to dangers. The following points are also worthy of consideration:

There are some matters which only develop after sufficient accumulation of information and opinions over the course of time. If we think about how mutual assistance is required to lift a large rock, we can understand this point easily. However, mutual support and assistance have no role in some other matters; for example, it is of no use for people to support or help each other in order to jump across a gorge. Some sciences need mutual support and assistance to develop. The majority of these are physical sciences. Mutual support has almost no use in other disciplines, such as

---

6   Abu 'Ali ibn Sina (Avicenna) (980–1037): One of the foremost philosophers, mathemat-
      cians, and physicians of the golden age of Islamic tradition. In the West, he is also known
      as the "Prince of Physicians" for his famous medical text *al-Qānūn* "The Canon" In Lat-
      in translations, his works influenced many Christian philosophers, most notably Thomas
      Aquinas. (Trans.)

attainment of intuitive knowledge of God or spiritual progress. Opinions brought forward, one after the other, through history do not change their nature, but rather add to arguments and serve for clarification.

It is also important that one who is much occupied in a subject is usually more insensitive to other subjects and cannot understand these so well. For this reason, those who are greatly occupied in physical or material matters lack sufficient knowledge or have only superficial understanding of spiritual matters. Therefore, such people's opinions and judgments concerning spiritual matters carry no weight. If a patient confounds medicine with engineering and decides to seek advice from an engineer rather than a physician, it means he has preferred to move to the hospital of the grave or sent his relatives an early invitation to send condolences on his death. Similarly, applying to materialists or consulting their opinion in matters of spirituality, which are usually abstract, means that the heart, which is a faculty of faith and spirituality, will go into arrest while the intellect, which is a spiritual faculty, will atrophy. It is true that those who search for every truth in corporeality have their intellects in their corporeal senses, when corporeal senses are blind to spiritual things.

The Third Premise

Some of the borrowings from the earlier non-Islamic, particularly Israelite, sources and ancient Greek philosophy infiltrated the sphere of pure Islam and, donning religious apparel, caused revolutions in some minds.

The Arabs were largely an illiterate people during the age of pre-Islamic ignorance. When the truth manifested itself among them, arousing their abilities, they saw that Islam was clear in itself and that the truth had been revealed, opening the way to the entire truth; as a result, their efforts and inclinations were focused on learning the Religion. Their observation of the universe was not in the name of scientific investigation, but rather for the purpose of finding evidence for the truth of their faith. What appealed to their natural tastes and inspired them was their awe-inspiring natural environment, and what motivated, informed and trained their talented natures was the Qur'an. However, when they later began to take other peoples into their community, the information that came with these peoples became "Muslim." In particular, the conversion of some Jewish scholars, such as Wahb ibn Munabbih[7] and Ka'b al-Ahbar,[8] caused some excerpts from Israelite sources to find their way into the minds of the Arabs and polluted their way of thinking. In addition, these borrowings received unconditional welcome from people because such scholars from among the People of the Book enjoyed great respect as they had converted and earned renown as Muslims. Since in appearance these borrowings were not contradictory to the fundamentals of Islam and circulated in the form of narratives, they were accepted uncritically. Unfortunately, they later came to be accepted as criteria for certain truths and for understanding some verses of the Qur'an, giving rise to many doubts and misunderstandings.

These excerpts from Israelite sources could be used to understand some implications of the Qur'an and Sunna. But they could never be taken as meanings or interpretations of the Qur'anic verses and Prophetic Traditions. Provided they were true, a place could be found for them in meanings of a secondary, even a third or fourth, degree. However, those who concentrated only on the literal meanings of the Qur'anic verses and who were lacking in, or did not look for, reliable sources to understand the verses, attempted to interpret some Qur'anic verses, as well as some Prophetic Traditions, in the light of the Israelite narratives. By contrast, what reliably interprets the Qur'an is primarily the Qur'an itself and the reliably narrated Hadith.[9] Neither the Torah nor the Gospels, whose legal rules and decrees had been abrogated and narratives distorted, can be used to interpret the Qur'an. The suggestions and connotations of the (words and images employed in some) Qur'anic verses and Prophetic Traditions cannot be taken as the underlying or essential meanings (to which those words and images allude) but, in some cases, people did take certain suggestions or

---

[7]   Wahb ibn Munabbih (654–737?) was one of the earliest Muslim traditionists. Well-versed in Jewish traditions, according to some, he was of Jewish origin. He was mostly influenced by 'Abdullah ibn 'Abbas, one of the famous, most knowledgeable Companions of the Prophet, upon him be peace and blessings. (Trans.)

[8]   Ka'b al-Ahbar (?–653) was previously a Jewish Rabbi from Yemen. He accepted Islam after the death of the Prophet, upon him be peace and blessings. He was criticized for narrating *Isra'iliyat* (borrowings from Israelite sources). (Trans.)

[9]   As commonly accepted, Hadith denotes the record of whatever Prophet Muhammad, upon him be peace and blessings, said, did, or tacitly approved. It is the collection of the Prophetic Traditions. (Trans.)

connotations as the true meanings, and so likelihoods or possibilities were presented as if they were the underlying or essential meaning.

A time came during the reign of Caliph Ma'mun[10] when some works from ancient Greek philosophy were translated in order to "Islamize" that philosophy. Thus, that philosophy, which is based to some degree on a wide variety of myths and superstitions and thus had been contaminated to a certain degree, was mixed with the pure thinking of the Muslim Arabs and, in its relation to those foreign works, caused imitation to replace verification to certain extent.

Although the Arabs were knowledgeable and intelligent enough to infer the meanings and rules they needed from the pure, sufficient sources of Islam, they lowered themselves to become students of Greek philosophy. Fortunately, in the same way as the Muslim linguists who had exerted themselves to establish and put into writing the rules of the Mudar dialect of Arabic when that dialect, the origin of the Arabic language, showed signs of corruption when non-Arab peoples entered the fold of Islam, meticulous truth-seeking scholars of Islam attempted to purify Islam of the corrupt elements of Greek philosophy and the false borrowings from Israelite sources, when these began to seep into the sphere of Islam. Despite their considerable success, some of those elements and borrowings remained and were not eliminated. In addition, when great, praiseworthy efforts began to be concentrated on the interpretation of the Qur'an, some of those who restricted themselves to the literal meanings of the verses tried to reconcile the narratives in the Qur'an with borrowings from related material in the Israelite sources, as well as trying to interpret some intellectual questions in the terms drawn from ancient Greek philosophy. They saw that the Qur'an and Hadith address and satisfy both the heart and the intellect, and contain the whole of the revealed knowledge. Thus, they attempted to find conformity between purely religious matters in the Qur'an and the Hadith and the Israelite reports, which were in fact corrupted and distorted. Since they also imagined there to be some sort of agreement between some intellectual questions in the Qur'an and the

---

10   Abu Ja'far al-Mu'min ibn Harun al-Rashid (786–833) was one of the most famous 'Abbasid Caliphs. He ruled from 813 until his death. He founded *al-Bayt al-Hikma* (The House of Wisdom) where especially Greek philosophy and sciences were translated into Arabic. (Trans.)

Hadith and ancient Greek philosophy, they tried to apply the latter also to the interpretation of the Qur'an and the Hadith.

This was indeed the wrong way. The Qur'an is a miraculous Divine Word; it cannot be imitated and no one can produce even a single verse that resembles it. So first of all, the matter should be approached from this point. What will interpret the Qur'an is itself—its own sentences, expressions, and phrases. Its meaning is in and of itself, like a pearl in an oyster. Even if one intended to declare the truth and excellence of the Qur'an through an imagined agreement between the Qur'an and Greek philosophy, again, it would be pointless. The Book, which is clear in itself and reveals all truth, is far removed from needing to be proven by such rational and reported knowledge, which itself is in need of the Qur'an to be proven and accepted. Conversely, if the Qur'an does not prove that knowledge, its testimony would not be worthy of attention. The Pleiades should be searched for in the sky, not on the earth. So too, you must search for the meaning of the Qur'an in the Qur'an, in its wording. Do not search for it in your pocket, where everything is jumbled together. You cannot find it there; even if you think you have found it, the Qur'an does not accept this because such verification does not bear the stamp of its eloquence.

It is among the accepted facts of eloquence that what we call meaning is that which penetrates the mind and heart when the wording has poured into the ears, and then is absorbed by the inner intellect, which causes it to open into flowers of thought. So, if you take for the meaning of the Qur'anic verses and the Prophetic Traditions those thoughts that have sprung up in your mind because of your preoccupation with other things and if you add to that what you have stolen from the false elements of philosophy and some fictitious narratives, attempting to introduce them as the true meaning of the Qur'an or Hadith, the answer you will receive is thus: "What you present as meaning is false. One who knows the genuine from the false will reject it. Something that is miraculous throughout, as the Qur'an is, rejects whoever has counterfeited it. Since you have attempted to destroy the order of the Qur'anic verses and the Prophetic Traditions, the verses will complain about you and the judge of eloquence will imprison your whims in your imagination. Any truth-seeking customers will not buy your counterfeit goods. They will tell you, 'The meaning of a verse is a pearl, but what you present as the meaning is a pebble. The meaning of a Tradition engenders life like a spirit, but yours is something very ordinary!'"

AN EXAMPLE TO CLARIFY

It is narrated among the Kurds: A man who stole honey was warned that his theft would be discovered. Upon this, he filled a hive with bees that did not produce honey, and stored in it the honey he stole from other hives. When asked about the honey, he would say, "This is the honey produced by my bees," and he would say to his bees, "You do the buzzing and I will provide the honey."

O one who attempts to interpret the Qur'an wishfully! Do not console yourself with this analogy with a theft on some pretext that you are not the only one who steals. Besides, the meaning you give to the Qur'anic verses is not honey, it is poison. The words you attempt to interpret are the words of that perfect Book, which inspires the spirits of truth in the heart and conscience. Those words are like angels. As for the Prophetic Traditions, they are a mine of truth and inspire the truth.

In short, just as going to one extreme is harmful, going to the opposite extreme is also harmful; in fact, it is even more harmful. However, going to one extreme is the greater fault, as this causes others to go to the opposite extreme. Such extremes have opened the door to tolerance for any interpretation, and unsound things have become mixed with sublime Qur'anic truths. This has led some unfair critics, and those who tend to go to extremes to accuse the Qur'an and the Prophetic Tradition of containing certain fallacies. They have horribly wronged these two priceless sources of Islam and genuine sources of truths. If some counterfeit coins have become mixed into a treasure of precious coins, or some rotten apples fallen into an orchard from a neighboring one, is it fair or just to claim that the whole treasure consists of counterfeit coins or that the orchard only has rotten apples and reject it altogether?

CONCLUSION

What I would wish to conclude from this premise is the following: Common opinion demands a new interpretation of the Qur'an. Each age has characteristics peculiar to itself and therefore has its own needs and demands. Time adds its own interpretation, and new events and developments cause many new meanings to be discovered. What now prevails is scientific public opinion. So, I declare that there should be convened a "parliament of scientists" that would consist of specialists in natural and religious sciences. This parliament should bring into being a new interpretation of the Qur'an, without at all neglecting to make reference to the classical interpretations. They should work on the acceptable elements in these, deepening and developing them. We are living under a constitutional regime, so we should follow the principle of consultation in every matter. Public opinion is an observer. The consensus of scholars on a matter is a source of legislation in Islam. Thus, this principle confirms my thesis.

The Fourth Premise

Fame attributes to one something that one does not own.

It is a characteristic of humanity that in order to show something that is not known as noble or valuable, it is attributed to one who is famous for having or doing similar things. In other words, in order for any words, actions, or attitudes to be justified or at least not discredited, people attribute them to a famous person. They even attribute to that single one some good thing belonging to a whole nation. However, that person will reject that gift which is wrongfully attributed to him. For if an artist who is famous for a form of art or a particular skill and able to see what is beyond the apparent beauty is shown something that does not have any artistic beauty and is told that it belongs to him—an act which means wronging this person in the eyes of others—he will reject it with contempt. Yet, in accordance with the rule that the existence of something requires the existence of all of its parts, in order to find an excuse for the image, people try to attribute this artwork to that person in order to demonstrate that that person truly possesses whatever has been attributed to him; people will also assign to this person exceptional abilities, such as extraordinary greatness, power, and intelligence. Thus this person takes on a superhuman form in the minds of people. If you want an example, look at the image of Zaloglu Rustem[11] in

---

[11] Zaloglu Rustem is an Iranian mythical hero who can be seen as the counterpart of the R - man Hercules or the Greek Heracles. (Trans.)

the minds of Iranians. Since he was famous for his bravery, his persona has been blown out of all proportion; to him has been attributed almost anything that is a cause of pride for the Iranians. As one lie usually leads to another lie, such great bravery appropriates to itself a life filled with other extraordinarily praiseworthy accomplishments, a very high, admirable stature, and many other laudable characteristics. Reflected as an imposing image on the wall across from the fire of imagination in which it was fed, the image says, "I am a person who represents all my people; I am even a whole people manifested as a single person." Such an approach adds to itself many legends and is circulated among the people, the image growing as strange as an ogre. Such tales cause other tales conformable to it to appear.

O you who want to see this reality in all its clarity! Pay attention to this premise, for the door to false beliefs opens with the reality explained here, while the door to verification is closed by it. Also, the courage to invent new things and develop new opinions based on the essentials of the Religion, as recorded in the classical works of the scholars of the earliest times, is lost in this wasteland. If you like, ask Molla Nasreddin Efendi,[12] "Do all those humorous anecdotes and sayings attributed to you really belong to you?" He will answer, "All those anecdotes and sayings comprise volumes. Saying and experiencing all of that would take a very long life. Besides, whatever I have said and done is not humorous and wise. If you assigned one fortieth of this to me, it would be enough. I do not want the rest, for the rest changes my natural and proper subtlety into something artificial."

Thus, from this root many false beliefs and myths grow like weeds and stifle the power of truths.

CONCLUSION

Attributing to anything or anyone more good than God has attributed to them is not a positive move, nor does it mean that you have done them any good. A single grain of truth is preferable to a bumper harvest of false imaginings. We must be content with defining something or someone with

---

12   Molla Nasraddin or Nasreddin Khodja was a thirteenth-century Muslim religious figure who was famous and remembered for his wisdom, legendary wit, funny stories and anecdotes. (Trans.)

the good God has accorded them in creation and the virtues they have. Anything that enters a community should not destroy the order of the community. The honor of a thing lies in itself, not in its lineage. Fruit displays the nature and quality of the roots. Any produce, no matter how valuable it is, added to someone else's produce usually damages the latter's worth, and may even cause it to be sequestrated.

Based on all these criteria, I say: It is sheer ignorance and a great fault to attribute some fabricated Traditions to the distinguished Companions, such as 'Abdullah ibn 'Abbas[13] in order to encourage people to do the religious acts or to discourage them from indulging in prohibited things. Truth is "wealthy" enough not to need such attributions, and its light is enough to illuminate hearts. Authentic Traditions are sufficient for us to interpret the Qur'an, and we are content with accurate narratives weighed on the scales of reason.

The Fifth Premise

When passing from the hands of knowledge to the hands of ignorance, a metaphorical expression may change into a literal description and open a door to superstition. Thus, whenever the dark hand of ignorance usurps a metaphor or simile from the luminous hand of knowledge, it may be taken for a reality. Also, whenever a metaphor or simile enjoys a long life, it loses its freshness and taste. Just as a handsome youth may, with the passage of time, become old and ugly, so too a metaphor or simile, once a source of fresh drinking water, may become, with the passage of time, a deceiving mirage.

The transparency of a metaphor displays the glint of truth. But if a metaphor is taken for a reality, it then becomes dense and masks the truth it is meant to display. Actually, this change is something that has taken place throughout history and so can be regarded as natural. Consider how a language undergoes changes over the course of time. Since many words, expressions, narratives, and meanings that were addressed to the comprehension of earlier generations have gradually grown old and lost their lus-

---

13   'Abdullah ibn 'Abbas (619–687) was a cousin of Prophet Muhammad, upon him be peace and blessings. He was extraordinarily well-versed in Qur'anic exegesis, as well as an authority on the Sunna of the Prophet and Islamic Jurisprudence. (Trans.)

ter and attraction, new generations, which do not see them as suited to their appetites and tastes, dare to make changes in them or even coin new ones to replace them. This occurs not only in language but also in images, meanings, and narratives. This teaches us that we should not judge everything according to its appearance. One who searches for truth should be like a diver, freed of the effects of time, able to dive into the depths of the past, weigh ideas on the scales of reason, and discover the source of everything. What led me to this conclusion is the following event: once during my childhood there was an eclipse of the moon. I asked my mother about it. She answered that a snake had swallowed the moon. I asked why I could still see it then. She explained, "The snakes of the sky are semi-transparent."

See how a simile taken for a reality conceals the truth. For ancient astronomers the word "snake" referred to an indistinct shape that somewhat resembles a snake during the lunar eclipse. Over time the common people took this term of science, a simile to describe a reality, and thought that there really was in the sky a snake that sometimes swallowed the moon!

O you who are not tired of these jumbled words of mine! Pay attention to this premise! Look at it through a microscope. For it is the source of many superstitions and false beliefs. Thus, we should adopt reason and the sciences of rhetoric or linguistics as a guide.

CONCLUSION

A true meaning has the stamp of truth. This stamp in religious matters consists of the pure beauty formed by the accurate balance that is contained within the purposes of the Shari'a. Using metaphors is permissible provided they conform to the rules of rhetoric and linguistics. Otherwise, there is risk that we will interpret or use a metaphor as reality or vice versa. This adds to the oppressive power of ignorance. Going to extremes by considering everything to be a metaphorical usage and looking for the truth in the esoteric dimension of the words and making an esoteric interpretation of every verse, even giving rise to a school of esotericism, is harmful. On the other hand, going to the opposite extreme by making an exoteric interpretation and looking for the truth only in the literal meaning of the words is also harmful. The middle, safe way, which prevents going to extremes, is the spirit of Shari'a, that is, rhetoric, reason or logic, and wisdom.

Wisdom (which is based on the Prophetic practice of the Qur'an and also includes a rational approach to it) is pure good. There may be some mistakes in the rational human approach, but this does not detract much from the great good that is inherent in wisdom. It is an essential maxim affirmed by many that abandoning something in which there is greater good than evil is to commit a greater evil. Since in the past philosophy was polluted with superstition because of ignorance, blind imitation, and the narrow capacity of minds, the scholars of earlier generations urged that philosophy be avoided. However, philosophy embedded in and informed by reported knowledge based on the Divine Revelation, and which also takes into account scientific developments, will surely bring more good than evil.

The Sixth Premise

Anything that is in a book of Qur'anic interpretation is not necessarily included in the meaning of the Qur'an, nor in the interpretation itself. Knowledge enables and gives strength to more and other knowledge. No one should impose their opinion on others. It is among the self-evident realities that one who is a specialist in a discipline like engineering can be quite ignorant in another discipline like medicine. It is an established principle of the methodology of Islamic jurisprudence (fiqh) that one who is not a trained and qualified faqih—a jurist, a specialist in the Islamic Law—even though he may be an expert in the methodology of fiqh, is not counted among the faqihs. Such a person is only an ordinary person in relation to faqihs.

It is just a reality of life that a person cannot be expert in many disciplines. One with an extraordinary capacity may be expert at most in four or five branches of science. An attempt to obtain everything means abandoning much of everything. Every discipline has its own nature and form of subject matter and discourse, and specialization in it means being an embodiment of the nature and form of that science. If specialists in one branch do not use their extra general knowledge as a supplement to enrich their field of specialization, then what emerges from their knowledge will not be reliable, and may indeed be ludicrous.

A FICTITIOUS EXAMPLE TO CLARIFY

Let us suppose there is a painter who has come from another world. He has never seen a complete human being or any other creature from this world; he has seen only some parts of every creature. He wants to draw a complete picture of a human or another creature. If he drew a human picture from a single hand, a foot, an eye, an ear, or only one side of the face, the nose, or a turban, or if he were to attempt to draw a picture of an animal with the tail of a horse, the neck of a camel, the face of a human being, and the head of a lion, people would ridicule him, saying, "Such a creature could not possibly live in our world."

This is true for all branches of science; therefore we should specialize in one branch and make our general knowledge like a pool from which we assist the study of that branch. It is also a reality that knowledge of various kinds and on various topics can be found in a single work. For sciences help and support one another and form such a complex network that questions related to the main theme of the work may sometimes be less important than the other questions discussed in it. Unaware of this reality, when a demagogue, or one whose understanding is restricted to and content with the literal meaning of the Qur'anic wording, sees a matter alluded to in a book of the Shari'a or of Qur'anic interpretation, he may remark, "The Shari'a or the Qur'an says this so." If that person is a friend of Islam, they may conclude, "One who does not accept this cannot be a Muslim." If an enemy, they may say (God forbid!), "The Shari'a or the Qur'an is in error."

O those who move from one extreme to the other, the meaning of the Qur'an and the Shari'a are not identical with the books written about them. A book is like a shop; even if it is a jewelry shop, there may be some worthless things in it alongside the valuable ones. Just as we cannot buy the materials necessary for the construction of a house from a single manufacturer, but must apply to the manufacturers of many different goods and the many different tools used by different building trades, so too we should expect to act appropriately when considering the meaning of the Qur'an, which is a palace of perfections. If your watch is broken and you go to the tailor to get it fixed, what will the result be?

AN INDICATION

This premise is founded upon the fact that God has established the law of development towards perfection, applicable to both the creation and the life of the universe. He is pleased with the division of labor that occurs when this law is followed. Acting in compliance with this principle of division of labor is compulsory upon every individual; yet we have not fully observed it. It is as follows:

The Divine wisdom which requires a division of labor has sown different abilities and tendencies in human nature, and has enabled human beings to carry out the duty of establishing sciences and developing technology. The fulfillment of this duty is obligatory upon humanity as a whole, though not on every individual. However, as Muslims, we have misused these abilities and tendencies, and have dampened the zeal which gives strength to our tendencies with inappropriate, destructive ambitions and the desire to be superior to others, which is the source of ostentation. Evidently, one who rebels deserves hellfire. So, as we have not observed the Divine laws of creation and the operation of the universe, we suffer the hellfire of ignorance as a punishment. What will save us from this torment is observing the law of the division of labor. The generations that preceded us observed this and subsequently rose to the heaven of knowledge.

CONCLUSION

It is not enough for a non-Muslim, in order to become a Muslim, merely to enter a mosque. Likewise, merely by being included in books of Shari'a or interpretations of the Qur'an, matters pertaining to the natural sciences or to philosophy, geography, history, and so on, cannot be regarded as being included in matters of the Shari'a or the Qur'an. Also, only when they are specialists in their fields can interpreters of the Qur'an or jurists have a definitive say in the interpretation of the Qur'an or jurisprudence, respectively. Their opinions on the matters parenthetically included in the books of these sciences are not to be regarded as definitive evidence or rulings. Furthermore, they may be borrowings. Now, those who convey borrowings are not to be reproached for that. But relying on reports or borrowings from sources of other sciences to construct definitive evidence or rulings in a certain science, just because they have been taken from experts in those other sciences, means falling into disagreement with the Divine

law of division of labor, the law of assigning to everyone a task to which
they are entitled or in which they are specialized.

Also, it is a principle in logic that a conclusion from a text is built
upon the relationship between the main theme of that text and the underlying meaning that it carries. Further studies of the text and additional
explanations do not necessarily have to be based on or originate from the
science which gives rise to the text. They can be related to other sciences
with which the text has some connection.

It is widely accepted that an expression employed to convey a general
meaning does not necessarily constitute an argument or proof for some particular meaning incidental to that general meaning or alluded to or required
by it.[14] For example, the famous interpreter Qadi Baydawi[15] holds that the
steep mountains mentioned in the verse—*[Dhu'l-Qarnayn said:] "Bring me
blocks of iron."* *Then, after he had filled up [the space between] the two steep
mountain-sides, he said: "[Light a fire and] work your bellows!" At length, when
he had made it [glow red like] fire, he said: "Bring me molten copper that I may
pour upon it"* (18:96)—are the mountains of Armenia and Azerbaijan. It
would be unreasonable and illogical to accept this opinion of a great interpreter as the final truth. What led to him to this opinion was information
he received from other sciences. The Qur'an is silent about which mountains those mentioned were. So, Baydawi's reading cannot be included as
falling within the meaning of the Qur'an itself. But it would also be unjust
to criticize this illustrious interpreter or shed doubt on his profound knowledge and comprehension in the science of Qur'anic interpretation because
of this reading. One should accept it as one expert's opinion but realize that
other opinions are also possible.

---

[14] An expression can convey meaning in three ways: 1. It can give the meaning of just what it
says. 2. It can give or allude to a secondary meaning. 3. It can (directly or indirectly) require
another meaning by implication. For example, the sentence, "Zakah is given to poor Muslims," meaning just what it says, tells us that Zakah is given to those Muslims who are poor.
It means secondarily that Zakah is not given to those Muslims who are wealthy. It can also
be understood to require the meaning that anybody who is not poor and not Muslim cannot
be given Zakah. (Trans.)

[15] Nasir al-Din Abu'l-Khayr 'Abdullah ibn 'Umar al-Baydawi (d. 1286) is one of the greatest
commentators of the Qur'an. He is author of many works on a number of subjects including Qur'anic interpretation, jurisprudence, law, and theology. His most famous work is his
commentary on the Qur'an, Anwaru't-Tanzil wa Asraru't-Ta'wil ("The Lights of the Divine
Revelation and the Mysteries of Its Meaning"). (Trans.)

The basic truths in the Qur'an and the Shari'a are clear. They shine as brightly as the stars. The clarity and power those truths possess give an incompetent like me encouragement to declare that every truth of the Qur'an and the Shari'a is based on and results in a decisive reality, and that it is weighed on the scales of wisdom.

The Seventh Premise

Exaggeration causes disorder. That is, it is characteristic of human beings that, since they tend to magnify the pleasure they receive from something, inflate what they are describing, and use exaggeration in their narratives, they mix reality with the imagination. Even if one intends to do good, to act in this way is in fact doing an evil or harmful thing. What they call reform becomes deforming, and what they consider as good and praiseworthy is in fact evil and disparaging. Such behavior unknowingly destroys the beauty that arises from balance and proportion. Just as taking a higher dose of medicine than is required simply because it tastes good or makes one feel good turns something that is beneficial into something harmful, exaggeration intended to encourage or discourage, despite the fact that the truth does not require this—for example, regarding backbiting as being as sinful as murder, or urination while standing as great a sin as unlawful sex, or deeming a few dollars of charity as meritorious as carrying out pilgrimage, in fact means that the crimes of murder and unlawful sex have lost some of their gravity and pilgrimage has been degraded. For this reason, a preacher should be wise and judicious and exercise reasonableness. Preachers devoid of these qualities have caused many religious truths to be sullied. For instance, the additional reports concerning the Prophet's miracle of splitting the moon[16] that one part of the moon descended into his pocket only darken this dazzling miracle, which is as bright as the sun in proving

---

[16] Prophet Muhammad, upon him be peace and blessings, split the moon by a gesture of his index finger as a miracle he worked before a group of people who rejected his Prophethood in Makka. It was related by the most authentic Hadith sources such as *Sahih al-Bukhari*, *Sahih Muslim*, and *Sunan at-Tirmidhi*. The verses, *The Last Hour has drawn near, and the moon has split. Whenever they see a miracle, they turn from it in aversion and say: "This is sorcery like many others, one after the other."* (54:1–2) refer to this miracle. For a discussion about this miracle, see, Ali Ünal, *The Qur'an with Annotated Interpretation in Modern English*, The Light, New Jersey, 2008, pp. 1082–1083. (Trans.)

Muhammad's Prophethood, and provide arguments to those who deny that it occurred.

In short, whoever loves the Religion and truth should be content with the original value and proportion of everything and not go beyond that through exaggeration. Such exaggeration means slandering the Divine Power and being discontent with the beauty and perfection that exists in creation; such behavior led Imam al-Ghazali[17] to say, "It is not probable that there could be a universe more beautiful than the present one."

O my readers! A parable or comparison sometimes serves the same purpose as evidence. If so, listen! Just as each of the metals, like diamond, gold, silver, lead, and iron has a value and characteristic particular to itself and just as each is different from the others, in the same way the basic purposes the Religion pursues are not identical with one another in value or in the requirement of evidence. While one of them finds a place for itself in the mind, the other finds a place in the conscience, while still another nestles in the innermost faculties of the human being. One who pays a diamond or a piece of gold for something worth ten cents is judged to be a foolish profligate and banned from trade. Even if this is not a formal legal judgment, such a person is reproached and regarded as a silly dreamer instead of being respected as a wise trader. In the same way, those who cannot distinguish between the religious truths or assign to each its value and proportion, and those who cannot recognize the stamp of the Shari'a on all of its rules and decrees, those who impede the movement of every part in that magnificent, heavenly factory, resemble a naïve person who goes to a huge, marvelously well-organized factory and sees there a tiny wheel. To his superficial view this tiny wheel seems to be out of keeping with the great wheels; it cannot possibly be as important or vital. He not only has no knowledge of mechanical engineering, he is also very conceited. In order to improve the workings of the factory, according to his superficial view, he replaces that tiny wheel with something more imposing. But

---

[17] Imam al-Ghazali, Abu Hamid Muhammad (d. 1111): A major theologian, jurist, and sage who was considered a reviver (of the religious sciences and Islam's purity and vitality) during his time. Known in Europe as Algazel, he was the architect of Islam's later development. He left behind many books, the most famous being *Ihya' 'Ulum al-Din* ("Reviving the Religious Sciences"). (Trans.)

the result is that he destroys the delicate working balance in the factory, causing great harm.

In short, on every rule and decree of the Shari'a there is a stamp of value particular to it, which has been placed there by the One Who established the Shari'a. This stamp should be read carefully. Each of those rules and decrees, the value of which is exhibited by the stamp, is far beyond needing any additional value to be given to it. It is also far removed from needing any exaggerated descriptions by those who are fond of exaggeration and verbosity, who think that they are making them valuable. Such people should be careful about how ugly they appear in the sight of the truth. A person of that kind once uttered a monstrous thing to a group of people—with the intention of discouraging drinking alcohol—but I am embarrassed even to write about it. Such people should know that they do the Shari'a great harm by such actions. Even if they mean to acts as friends of the Shari'a, they can at best be regarded as foolish friends, and such people may be much more harmful to the Shari'a than its enemies.

CONCLUSION

O unfair ones who are outside the fold of Islam and attempt to criticize it from afar! Do not be deceived, use your reason, and do not be content with superficial views. Those who provide you with pretexts to criticize Islam are called evil scholars in the language of the Shari'a. Look beyond the veil they have formed with their imbalance and self-restriction to the outer aspect of the Religion and the literal meaning of the Qur'an and the Traditions. You will see that every truth of Islam is as bright as a shining star and that it is self-evident. Such truths bear the stamp of eternity. This is so because the Shari'a comes from the Eternal Speech of God—eternal in the past and eternal in the future. But unfortunately, factors such as egotism, self-centeredness, the inability to comprehend the truth, and seeing oneself as infallible, cause people to blame their own faults on others. They wish to show themselves as blameless by ascribing their words or acts that are likely to be incorrect to a renowned person or an accredited book or even to the Religion or a Prophetic Tradition or, finally, to Divine Destiny. God forbid such attitudes! Darkness does not emerge from light.

Even if a person conceals the stars in their own mirror, they cannot hide the stars in the sky. They can only hide the stars from themselves.

O you who oppose Islam! Like a child who tries to find an excuse for crying or a vengeful enemy who wants to take revenge, it is horribly unfair to try to stain Islam with the negative results that emerge in opposition to the Shari'a and the doubts that arise from misunderstanding. For it is almost impossible that every attribute and act of a Muslim can arise from Islam. (Everyone may be at fault and no religion should be blamed because of the wrongs some of its followers do.)

The Eighth Premise

AN ESTABLISHMENT

Do not tire of this long premise, for its conclusion is of great significance. Moreover, it defeats hopelessness, which destroys all perfections, and it vitalizes hope; it is the yeast of happiness in every matter. It also gives the glad tidings that the future will belong to the Muslims. It is about measuring the children of the past and the future.

The alphabet is not taught and studied in colleges. Even if knowledge has a definite, constant nature, it is taught in different ways. The school of emotions which we call the past is not the same as the university of thoughts called the future. What I mean by the children of the past is, in regard to non-Muslims, those who lived before the sixteenth century. As for the Muslims, they were very far ahead of all other peoples during the first three centuries of Islam, and during the succeeding two centuries they were more advanced, being revered in most matters. I call the subsequent seven centuries the past, and the time that follows the future.

What generally directs a person is either the reason or the sense-perceptions. In other words, people are directed either by their thoughts and emotions, or by right and force, or by wisdom and power, or by guidance or lusts and caprices. We see from this perspective that untainted but untrained tendencies and emotions were dominant in the children of the past and these directed their unenlightened thoughts. This sometimes caused divergences or conflicts. But since the enlightened opinions of the children of the future will hopefully dominate their emotions, which are darkened by desires, ambitions, and lusts, we can say with certainty that in the future law will prevail and humanity will manifest itself to a certain extent. In turn, this gives the glad tidings that Islam, which is the true and greatest humanity, will shine like an unclouded sun in the heavens of the future and over the orchards and gardens of Asia.

What generally prevailed in the past and gave rise to spite, enmity, and the complex of being superior was emotions, inclinations, and force. A powerful, convincing speech was enough to guide people. At that time, the ability to embellish a thesis in such a way that it would affect the feelings and inclinations or make it attractive with the power of rhetoric or gestures served for evidence. But comparing ourselves to them means returning to the corners of that time. Every age has a character peculiar to itself. We demand evidence, and are not deceived through the mere statement or embellishment of a thesis.

The source from which established truths originate, like vapor formed over the ground of the present to pour as rain on the mountains of the future, consists of thought, reason, right, and wisdom; and any thesis or claim put forward can only be proved through evidence, which gives rise to a tendency towards investigation, the love of truth, a preference for public interest over personal interest, and the awakening to truth of humanity. We are people of the present and candidates for the future. The embellishment of the thesis or a mere statement of it is not enough to satisfy our minds. We demand evidence.

Now, let us briefly mention the positive and negative aspects of the past and future. Since force, desires, natural untrained dispositions, and emotions were considerably dominant in countries of the past, despotism and authoritarianism prevailed. Enmity towards the way of others was more popular than love of one's own way. Enmity towards a person was manifested as friendship to that person's enemies. In addition, partisanship and fanaticism prevented the appearance of the truth. Since differences of opinion supported by partisanship caused fierce conflicts, the truth retreated and concealed itself. As one of the evils of despotism, what sustained the way of each and every group was generally bigotry and/or denouncing others as deviant or fallacious. Whereas, as all of these have attitudes that are condemned in the sight of the Shari'a, they are also contrary to religious brother/sisterhood, to the bonds of humanity, and the mutual assistance that is required by collective life. It sometimes even happens that when people have abandoned bigotry or its fallacies and entered on the way followed by people in unison, they have had to change their own way. However, if they had supported the truth instead of bigotry, followed evidence instead of fallacies, lived with love of their own way according to the rules of Shari'a and for the good pleasure of God instead of denouncing others as deviants, and had based their actions on consultation, they would not have felt the need to change their own way. But just as doubt and suspicion had no effect on people's minds during the Age of Happiness and the subsequent periods of the righteous generations due to the dominance of the truth and the application of evidence, reason, and consultation, so too, through the efforts of scientific thought and investigation will the truth prevail over force, evidence over fallacies, reason over disposition, guidance over lust and caprice, steadfastness in the truth over bigotry or fanaticism, public spirit over spite, intellectual tendencies over the inclinations of the carnal soul, thought over emotions. This will happen to some extent in the present and fully in the future. The situation was completely thus in the first three centuries of Islam and to a certain extent during the succeeding two centuries. From the sixth century onwards, everything began gradually to deteriorate.

It is one of the laudable effects of the dominion of thought that the sun of the truth of Islam has begun gradually to appear from behind the clouds of whims and imaginings and illuminate everything. Even those who have rotted in the swamp of unbelief are benefiting. It is the beauty of consultation that the ways followed and methods applied are founded on evidence and the facts are bound to the unchanging truth, leading to perfection in every field. As a result of this, falsehood will not be able to guide under the guise of truth and deceive minds.

O Muslim brothers and sisters! The present gives us the glad tidings that the reality announced in *The truth has come and falsehood has vanished* (17:81) has begun to show itself and, pointing to the future, announces with a loud voice: The truth of Islam, which is the representation of eternal justice in this world, will dominate over time and over the nature of humanity until the end of time, which is fast approaching. It is the greatest, true humanity.

The beauty brought by new developments in human civilization is an indicator of the dominance of the truth of Islam. Is it not apparent that owing to the intellectual enlightenment—a result of reasoned thoughts built one upon the other over the course of time—that the dust of whims and caprices which has been collected on the shoulders of Islamic truths has been partly eliminated? This suggests that these truths, which are the stars of the heavens of guidance, will appear fully in all their brightness and diffuse their light everywhere, even if their opponents struggle against this.

If you would like, go into the future and see how those who search for the truth of the Divine Oneness in Trinity in the field of truths under the supervision of wisdom and true knowledge attempt to struggle against those who have been girded with the sword of evidence and equipped with the true creed based on the Divine Oneness—the true creed that has been confirmed by sound intellects—see how they will be utterly defeated.

I swear by the wise styles of the Qur'an that what has thrown certain Christians into the valleys of misguidance, along with many others, is that they have dismissed reason, expelled evidence, and imitated the clerics blindly. What has allowed Islam to always manifest its excellences (despite all obstacles) and the truths to develop in accordance with the intellectual development of humanity is that Islam is based on the truth, it has equipped itself with evidence, it consults with reason, and does not conflict with the basic principles of scientific research, wisdom, or sound thinking. Is it not apparent that in many of its verses the Qur'an calls humanity to turn to their conscience and consult with their reason? The Qur'an frequently says: *Do they not contemplate...? Go about, then, on the earth and behold...! Do they not consider...? They reason and understand. They do not perceive. Then reflect...! Will you not, then, reflect and take heed? Learn a lesson, then, O people of insight! They know! They do not reason or understand.*

I say: Learn a lesson, then, O people of insight!

CONCLUSION

Learn a lesson, then, O people of insight! Do not restrict yourselves to or get stuck in what you see only with your eyes! The truth is waiting for you. But when you see it, do not damage it!

The Ninth Premise

It is a fact recognized by those of sound thinking and reason that in creation what is good is original, essential, all-inclusive, and prominent, and what is evil is derivative, and of a minor or second degree. We can elaborate on this as follows:

There is a branch of science that has been developed or is developing to study every species of creation. Each species has general characteristics of its own, and there are general principles that dominate its existence and govern its life; it can be said that the branch of science that studies each species consists of those general principles. That the principles are general exposes the beauty of the order in the life of that species. This means that all sciences bear true witness to the beauty of the order of the universe. The universal system, with its complete, organism-like structure, is a proof of this orderly beauty. If something does not have an order, there can be no general rule or principle for its existence. Many exceptions destroy the beauty of orderliness. The principle of induction (and the existence of the "general laws of nature") proves this thesis. However, sometimes we cannot see this universal order because of our incapacity to comprehend the whole of existence or even a species in its totality. This causes the universal order to not display itself in all its dimensions. Whereas, all of the "natural" sciences that are based on general rules or laws and the principle of induction prove that the basic and observable purpose for the creation of the universe is good, beauty, truth, and perfection. Evil, ugliness, and falsehood are superficial, derivative, and concocted. Even if they sometimes appear to prevail, this is temporary.

It is a fact that the most honorable and noble creation is humanity, and among humanity the people of truth are the most illustrious and honorable. As the truths of Islam bear witness to this, so too will future events bear it out. It is also a fact that the most perfect among existence in general and humanity in particular is Prophet Muhammad, upon him be peace and blessings. This is testified by his miracles, perfect morals, exceptional and unparalleled accomplishments, confirmed by verifying scholars and unbiased researchers and intellectuals, and also acknowledged even by many of his enemies.

In the face of all these established facts or truths, is it possible for humanity to annul the testimony of sciences through its incorrect acts and sinfulness, to falsify or destroy the order of existence which gives rise to the principle of induction; will they be able to resist the absolute Will of God? Will this ever be possible? I swear by the Names of the All-Merciful and the All-Compassionate, of the All-Just and All-Wise One that humanity will not be able to easily digest evil, ugliness, or falsehood. In addition, the Divine Wisdom will not allow this to be.

Aggression against the universal law is not forgiven, and its violation is not permitted. Even if evil were to prevail for numerous years, it would result in at least a thousand years of the victory of good. In addition, in the other world, good will eternally defeat evil and sentence it to eternal extinction. If this were not to be so, other species of creation obedient to the Divine laws of existence would not allow the unjust, wretched humankind to remain alongside them, and they would dismiss humankind from its duty in existence, expelling it to the darkness of non-existence. This would mean that the capacities granted to human beings and the abilities and tendencies with which they have been favored so that they could live a contented life in this world and be rewarded with eternal happiness in the Hereafter were all for nothing. Uselessness or futility is opposed both to the universal order and system, which enables the principle of induction, and to the Wisdom of the All-Wise Maker and the judgment of the truthful and trustworthy Prophet, upon him be peace and blessings. The future will eliminate some such baseless claims, and their complete elimination will occur in the Hereafter.

The prevailing of beauty and truth in existence will be victorious in the future. If we die, our nation will endure. We are not content with forty years of victory; we desire many more years. Nevertheless, the complete and eternal victory of beauty, right or truth, good, and perfection, whether on the individual or collective scale, will happen in the Hereafter, where humankind, like other species that are similar to it, will be punished or rewarded in proportion to their capacity and responsibility. For absolute truth and justice will rule and prevail there. This narrow world is not suitable for the infinite capacities that exist in the essence of human beings or their desires and inclinations that have been created for eternity to blossom in perfection. For this reason, they will be sent to another world where they will be perfected. Humanity has a lofty essence, an exalted nature, and so its crimes become tremendous also. Because of this, its education and obedience to the Divine universal laws are of great importance. It is not like other species. But, like other species, it should also obey the order of creation.

A being created for eternity is great, noble, and illustrious. It cannot be neglected or left to its own devices. It cannot be useless; it cannot be condemned to absolute non-existence, nor can it escape to it. Paradise and Hell are each awaiting their inhabitants; the former with its warm, welcoming arms, and the latter with its mouth wide open.

CONCLUSION

The future of Islam and the Muslim world appears bright, even from afar. For the following four or five irresistible forces work hand in hand for the victory of Islam, which has prevailed in our world for centuries.

The first force is the essential power of Islam, equipped with knowledge and true civilization.

The second is intense neediness or poverty, for the removal of which all means and prerequisites are available.

The third is the vigorous emulation and determined competitiveness, along with the hidden fervor which arise from seeing our world in misery and the world competing with it in prosperity, giving rise to an awakening and mobilization.

The fourth is the natural capacity equipped with unity in word and action, which is a principle belonging to believers in God's Oneness; and with moderation and composure, informed by the natural environment; and the intellectual enlightenment to which the present time has added; and the exchange and mutual support of ideas that are required by development and civilization; and the purity of disposition that arises from freedom from cultural contamination by modern sedentary life; and the simple lifestyle and endeavor that are necessitated by poverty.

The fifth is the duty of uplifting God's Word requiring material progress at the present time in particular; and the general tendency towards renewal and development which is equipped by the urge and force of Islam, the requirements of the time, the compulsion of poverty, and with a hope that is revitalized through the death of despair, a negative force that kills every craving and enterprise.

As a support for these five forces, the evils of modern civilization exceed its beauties—a factor that causes unrest among foreigners and makes that civilization grow old; labor is not sufficient for modern, dissipated life. These two developments occur for the following two reasons:

The first allows dissipation and submission to lust, while ignoring religion and virtue as the underlying foundations of civilizations.

The second is an excessive imbalance in living standards, caused by a lack of mercy that results from submission to lust and irreligious life. Indifference to religion in life has darkened the inner face of European civilization to the extent that it has given rise to many rebellious, anarchist groups. If they do not hold fast to the unbreakable cable of the Religion and the insurmountable barrier of the Divine way of life, those rebellious, anarchist groups will destroy their "civilized" world.

If the institution of the Zakah (the Prescribed Purifying Alms)—which is only one of the many substantive principles of the truth of Islam—is taken as one of the foundations of civilization and a rule for mutual help and solidarity, will it not be a cure for this affliction and for that nest of snakes, the alarming imbalance in living standards? Certainly, it is the perfect cure.

If it is asked why that which has secured the superiority of Europe to date will not continue to do so from now on, my reply is as follows:

First study the preface to this book, and then pay attention to what follows:

The reasons for the progress of Europe were the cold climate, which causes people to be tardy both in assimilating and in abandoning (major civilizational trends), and which inures them to hardships; the limited amount of land combined with high density of population, which urged people towards education and industrialization; and mutual helping and solidarity encouraged by the multiplicity of waterways and activities like mining, and the fact that they were surrounded by seas; and other similar factors. But today, the world is becoming a global town where a single community survives due to the developments in transportation and communication. In short, as their burden is heavy while ours is light, we will catch up with them and leave them behind, provided God comes to our aid.

A FINAL CONCLUSION

A constitutional regime and freedom will open the doors to a happy future for Islam and Asia, on condition that they follow the Religion.

A *warning*: The beautiful things that are found in civilization are, in fact, some elements of the Religion that have been given a new look.

The Tenth Premise

A speaker is not held accountable for all the meanings inferred by others from it. One is responsible for the meanings construed by others only if those meanings were intended. Otherwise, the speaker is not called to account. A speaker is responsible only for his intentions.

It is among the rules of the art of writing and speaking that truth and falsehood exist in the intention of the writer or speaker. As for the responsibility for the connotations and the meanings inferred by the listener, and the styles in use, these belong to customs or traditions. For customs or traditions have a role and are adhered to when conveying meaning. If the piece of writing criticized is a story, defects and faults are to be sought for in its heroes.

A speaker is not called to account for forms or connotations. For speakers do not stretch out their hands to them to pick their fruit, but rather they employ them to climb towards the branches of their main purposes. If you would like to, consider figurative or metaphorical accounts or descriptions. For example, they say in Turkey of generous people, "The sheath of so-and-so's sword is long and he himself has plenty of ashes," meaning the person talked about is rich and generous. Even if this person does not have a sword and ashes, we have still spoken the truth. Also consider the examples that begin with phrases like "Let's suppose" or "Supposing." As they have a value that arises from common usage, these phrases have the capacity to function as mediators in the exchange of views and consultation. Even the most exacting, truthful men of wisdom such as Jalal al-Din al-Rumi[18] and Sa'di al-Shirazi[19] did not

---

[18]   Mawlana Jalal al-Din al-Rumi (1207–1273): One of the most renowned figures of Islamic Sufism. Founder of the Mawlawi Order of the whirling dervishes, famous for his *Mathnawi*, an epic of the religious life in six volumes. For Western readers, Rumi is a powerful voice among the poets of Sufism. (Trans.)

[19]   Sa'di al-Shirazi (1215?–1292): The greatest didactic poet of Persia, author of the *Gulistan* ("Rose Garden") and the *Bustan* ("Orchard"), who also wrote many fine odes and lyrics. (Trans.)

see any fault in using them. If this truth has become visible to you, then light your candle by it, and go to the corners of narratives and stories. For anything valid for one part can sometimes be valid for the whole.

A REMINDER

In the Third Part, a basic principle will be mentioned concerning the firm, explicit, and allegorical expressions of the Qur'an. However, as I feel that it is necessary here, I will make a brief mention of it as follows:

God's primary purpose for sending His wise Book is the guidance of people. All human beings are not of the same level of understanding, nor are they specialists in every branch of science. Therefore, God speaks in His Scriptures in a way understandable to everyone. Those of a higher level of understanding and having expert knowledge can benefit from anything that is addressed to all people. But when a work addresses only the scholarly, things may become difficult for common people. Furthermore, people cannot easily abandon their habits or be freed from the things with which they have been familiar for a long time. People often find it hard to deal with abstractions, but find it easier to understand things when expressed with metaphors and similes as these are closer to everyday life. For this reason, truths are usually presented in familiar terms or forms and thereby effectively presented for guidance. However, we should not focus our views upon such forms. The Qur'an of miraculous exposition has considered how people can easily understand it and has used styles that are suitable to be presented in this way. The Qur'an is God's address to human beings in a form that they can understand. The following Qur'anic expressions are examples of this:

He has established Himself on the Supreme Throne (7:54).

God's Hand is over their hands (48:10).

Your Lord comes (89:22).

He saw it (the sun) setting in a spring of hot and black, muddy water (18:86).

The sun runs the course appointed for it (36:38).

That is how the Qur'an is, and there can be no doubt that it is God's Word.

CONCLUSION

An idea can be difficult to understand for two reasons. One is that it has been expressed in a poor style or in a poor language. The Qur'an is far above having such language or style. A different reason that may cause difficulties in understanding some Qur'anic expressions is that the Qur'an has profound, subtle, and multi-dimensional meanings. As the Qur'an is peerless in value and contains innumerable precious jewels, it does not uncover its secrets easily, but rather demands much care and concentration; the reason for, and the result of this, is that one is impelled and encouraged to study the Qur'an to find the deeper meanings it contains.

A REMINDER

As declared in a Prophetic Tradition, each Qur'anic verse has an outward and inward dimension of meaning, and every inward and outward dimension has a field of comprehensibility, with sub-domains in every field.[20] The religious sciences that have been established over the course of history bear witness to this fact. Every dimension or rank of meaning in each verse of the Qur'an has a particular, distinguishing merit, and this must be discovered. The ranks or dimensions of meaning do not cause confusion, but certain proximities in meaning can give rise to ambiguity or misunderstandings. In the same way that confusing the sphere we live in, where we must possess the necessary means or equipment to obtain a desired result, with the sphere of belief, where we attribute all effects to God's absolute Will, can cause either fatalism in the name of absolute reliance on God, or the deviation of attributing creativity to the created, similar results may appear if the ranks or dimensions of the meaning of a verse are not distinguished from one another.

The Eleventh Premise

There may be more than one judgment in a word. A single oyster may contain several pearls. In the same way it is a fact, realized by those with expert knowledge, that a text may contain more than one judgment. Each of these

---

[20]   Ibn Hibban, *Sahih,* 1:146; al-Munawi, *Fayd al-Qadir,* 3:54.

judgments arises from a different source and yields different fruit. One who cannot differentiate between them remains indifferent to and devoid of the truth. For example, a Prophetic Tradition says, "I and the end of the world are like these two fingers."[21] That is, the Prophet meant that there would be no Prophet after him. This Tradition contains three judgments:

ONE: This Tradition is attributed correctly to the Prophet, upon him be peace and blessings. This judgment is based on the reliability of the chains of transmission.

THE SECOND: The meaning expressed in this Tradition is true. This judgment is based on the evidence for the Prophethood of the Prophet, upon him be peace and blessings.

We must accept both of these judgments. One who denies the first commits a grave sin and is considered a liar. One who denies the second falls into misguidance and darkness.

THE THIRD: The judgment contained by the Tradition is what every qualified one deduces from it. One who has the necessary qualifications to deduce judgments from the Traditions says, "This is what was meant by this Prophetic saying; this is the pearl hiding in this oyster." This judgment cannot be reached through personal inclinations or desires or caprices. It should be based on true reasoning established on the necessary principles. One who is qualified to deduce a judgment from the Qur'an and the Prophetic Traditions (other than the explicit judgment[s] addressing and understandable by everyone) is not obliged to follow another with the same qualifications. Differences of view occur in this third judgment. Phrases such as "So-and-so says," and "It is said," which we frequently come across in relevant books, bear witness to that. Those who have the necessary qualifications to deduce judgments from the Qur'an and the Prophetic Traditions do not commit a sin when and if they disagree with the judgment of others. For the lack of a particular element or the non-acceptance of a personal judgment does not cause the invalidity of a whole or a general judgment. There are many statements that contain controversial judgments. For this reason, we should enter every house through its own door. Each house has a door of its own, and every lock a key of its own. (That is, we

---

21 Al-Bukhari, *al-Jami' al-Sahih*, "Riqaq" 39; Muslim, *al-Jami' al-Sahih*, "Fitan" 132–135; al-Tirmidhi, *Sunan*, "Fitan" 39.

should look at and accept the examples of this third type of judgment on the merits of each, tracing the process that brought the scholar to it.)

CONCLUSION

The three types of judgment mentioned concerning the Prophetic Traditions are also relevant to the Qur'anic verses. However, in respect to the first judgment, there is a slight but significant difference between the Qur'anic verses and the Prophetic Traditions. (There is no question that every verse of the Qur'an is absolutely part of it and that it has been revealed by God. Denial of any of these verses means unbelief.)

As pointed out at the beginning of this premise, there may be several other judgments in a word than the basic, intended one. However, they are of particular importance. Every one of these may issue from a different origin and bear a different fruit.

A REMINDER

Egotism and self-importance may give rise to some shameful and despicable attitudes, such as the intentional support of the opposing side, fanaticism, aspiring to be superior to others, unfair partisanship, exploiting a truth to justify an incorrect action, regarding weak points as being strong in favor of one's desires, attempting to show how virtuous one is by drawing attention to the defects of others, and demonstrating one's honesty and truthfulness by contradicting others or declaring them to be misguided. A person defeated by love of self or egotism can produce many excuses.

We should turn to God for deliverance from such base attitudes and behaviors.

The Twelfth Premise

One who cannot discover the kernel becomes occupied with and restricted to the shell. One who does not know the truth deviates into whims and fancies. One who cannot detect or find the straight path goes to extremes. One who does not have a true balance not only deceives others, but is greatly deceived.

One of the reasons for the deception of those restricted to the literal meaning of a text is their confusion of the narrative and the lesson found within it, as well as the closeness of the premise and the meaning intended by a text in the mind of the listener or reader. Please heed this point, for it is important.

An important reason that gives rise to chaos in opinions, which creates myths, superstitions, and exaggeration, is discontent with the beauty and magnificence in creation. It is trying to judge the order of existence with one's imperfect reason and knowledge, and thus demeaning it. In fact, the order, beauty, perfection, and magnificence in creation, each element of which is a miracle when perceived with sound reason and wisdom, are so apparent when compared with the beauty and perfection of those driven by dreams and fantasy that they appear in all their splendor and brilliance, without losing anything of their extraordinariness. It is everyday familiarity, which is a sister to multi-layered ignorance and the mother of superficial views that has blinded those fond of exaggeration. In order to open the eyes of such people, the Wise Book orders a careful observation of the facts in the human world, including physical composition, as well as an examination of the outer world. It is only the verses of the Qur'an that open eyes. These verses are stars with piercing lights; they remove the darkness of ignorance and superficiality, they rend apart the veils of everyday familiarity and restrictions to literal meanings, guiding intellects to the facts of the outer world and human inner world, and thus to the truth.

What prompts exaggeration is the natural tendency we have to realize our inclinations. A part of this tendency is that human beings innately desire to see and exhibit unusual things and invent new things. For this reason, when they do not feel the ever-original taste of the sustenance that feeds and satisfies the spirits in the universe, because obscured by superficial perception and everyday familiarity, they become tired of trying to lift the covering and the outer surface, and surrender to an appetite for rarity and "extraordinariness." This leads human beings to use exaggeration for the sake of novelty or to demand what is unusual. Like a snowball falling down a mountain-side, when exaggeration rolls from the highest summit of imagination down to the tongue and then from one tongue to another, it grows like an avalanche, while at the same time some parts are scattered around. The exaggeration grows so much that it fits neither into the heart nor the perceptive senses nor even the faculty of imagination. But later, a truth-seeing eye appears and uncovers all the extraneous parts, reducing that exaggeration to the original truth. Thus, the meaning of *The truth has come, and falsehood has vanished* (17:81) reveals itself.

A recent event can provide an illustration of this:

I have long tried to remove the stains that going to extremes has smeared on the truths of Islam, and striven to show those truths in all their brilliance. Recently I have clarified that Islam in no way opposes the obvious, long-established fact that the earth is spherical. On the contrary, Islam has many elements that support it. In doing so I have been able both to dismiss the objections of the enemies of Islam and remove the doubts of its friends. This matter will be explained in the section, *The Matters*. However, the minds of the literalists, which have long been accustomed to nightmares, seem discontented. It is as if they would like to make day into night by closing their eyes or by extinguishing the sun by blowing on it. They think that one who thinks that the earth is spherical opposes many truths of the Religion. Based on this supposition, they have slandered me. As they have found some fertile suspicious minds, they have gone so far in their slanders that they have caused much grief to people who are truly religious, as well as hopelessness in the hearts of some who are eagerly striving for the progress of Muslim peoples. This has provided me with an important lesson: an ignorant friend is as harmful as an enemy. Until this event, I had sought to break the extreme falsehoods of the enemies with the diamond sword of truth. Now I feel obliged to use this sword to a certain extent against the extreme whims of such friends. This is a matter which is important for understanding the present conditions of the religious schools in the East and if and how they are to be improved. I assure these literalists that their efforts are in vain. To date, they have aimed to win the applause of the common people and have caused our ignorance. They desire that we should remain ignorant and that they should continue to benefit from our ignorance. However, this can no longer be so, and religious schools truly need to be revitalized.[22]

---

22 Bediüzzaman Said Nursi criticizes here some of the contemporary scholars in the south-east of Turkey. (Trans.)

Another point that should be mentioned concerning the confusion in the minds of the literalists and the disorder in their imaginings is that they believe that the evidence for the truth of the Prophets consists only in their miracles. Because of this, they maintain that our Prophet, upon him be peace and blessings, was extraordinary in all his acts, attitudes, and states. Since this does not conform to reality, they have no order or balance in their thinking about him. This assertion derives from unawareness of the subtle truths of Divine Wisdom and the fact that, like all other people, the Prophets submitted and adhered to the Divine laws that operate in existence. Every act, word, and state of our Prophet shows his truthfulness and bears witness to his submission to the truth and that he followed the Divine laws and practices. This point will be discussed in the Third Part.

God creates miracles at the hands of the Prophets in order to demonstrate their Prophethood and to encourage people to affirm the same. The miracles every Prophet worked were sufficient to prove his Prophethood. To work miracles or display instances of extraordinariness beyond what is necessary would be pointless and contradict the responsibility that is a means of testing people with what they are expected to believe in. No one is invited to believe in something that is obviously undeniable. Such an invitation would be contrary to Divine wisdom in sending Prophets and Religions, and which tests people by their acceptance of or faith in what has been taught to them. Prophets are responsible for submission and obedience to the Divine wisdom first of all and to an extent greater than others.

O you who heed these inarticulate words of mine! The seeds of inclinations implanted in your nature will grow and flourish in the sun of the truth which appears in these Twelve Premises; this sun is at the same time mobile and stable.[23]

CONCLUSION

It is sinful to deny that one descends from the Prophet's Family; it is also a sin to claim to be a descendant of the Prophet's Family although one is not. In

---

[23] Here Said Nursi refers to the fact that the sun is both stable and mobile in itself and in its system, a fact which modern Astronomy discovered in 1993. See, M. Bartusiac, "Sounds of the Sun," *American Scientist* (Jan.–Feb. 1994): 61–68; Ali Ünal, "The Styles of the Qur'an and the Movement of the Sun," *Islamic Perspectives on Science*, The Light, New Jersey, 2007, pp. 155–159. (Trans.)

the same way, it is strictly forbidden to add to or subtract from the Qur'an and the Prophetic Traditions. Addition is more harmful, as it destroys the order and causes doubts and misconceptions, whereas ignorance may be an excuse for unintentional omission. Similarly, removing something from the Religion or making any addition to it is not permissible.

With the cheap coin of narratives, the rubbish of borrowings from earlier corrupted religions, and the pus of some similes, the diamond of the Islamic creed, the jewel of the Shari'a, and the pearls of the Islamic rules of life, have been devalued, discouraging and repulsing those who seek the truth.

A FINAL CONCLUSION

It would be in contradiction of the Divine laws of creation and life if a person were to abandon something for which they have a talent and attempt to do something which they are not qualified to do. Everyone is expected to develop their talents by applying them in a task for which they are qualified, following the rules of the craft or job at which they are skilled. Misuse of such talents and acting contrary to the rules of any craft or job causes distortion and corruption. Any incompatibility between a natural skill or capacity and a task performed will give rise to confusion. For this reason, many people who aspire to superiority and domination over others abuse knowledge, employing it as a force to exert their domination, despite the fact that knowledge and teaching require encouragement, the provision of guidance, advice, and gentleness. Even though people are expected to serve knowledge, some use it for their personal interests. This has caused many public offices to be occupied by those who are not qualified, leading to the near collapse of religious schools. Thus, we should follow the Divine wisdom in the creation of people with different talents, and apply the rule of the division of labor, encouraging a concentration on religious sciences so that everyone can study the subject they choose and for which they have an aptitude.

A REMINDER

An important cause of the degeneration of religious education and its distortion from its true course is this: The subordinate or instrumental scienc-

es (such as logic, linguistics, and philology) have been given more importance than the primary, exalted sciences (such as jurisprudence, Qur'anic
interpretation, and study of Hadith). The grammatical analysis of Arabic
texts has conquered minds, with the result that the study and knowledge
of the primary or basic sciences have been considerably neglected.

O brothers and sisters of conscience! It is my opinion that you would
like to see the nature of the matters to be discussed in the following lines
based upon the premises discussed. But I beg of you a little more time!
Here, I would like to present something that constitutes the core or out-
line of those matters. Then I will present ten matters for your perusal.

I will try to rise to the sciences of the heavens by the means provided
by the Qur'an and those sciences themselves. We will see that the All-
Wise Maker unceasingly turns the earth like a ball in His Hand of Power.
We will see with the eyes of wisdom that He can and will destroy it utterly and replace it with a new one. Then, traveling through the atmosphere,
we will land on the earth, which the All-Merciful Creator has made as a
couch or cradle for living beings, including humankind. Afterwards, we
will carefully observe that just as a person grows out of childhood and stops
lying in a cradle, humankind will destroy its cradle and be sent to the
world of eternity. After this observation, we will make a spiritual journey
beyond the restrictions of time and space, and enter the realm of the past,
communicating with its residents through the historical current of "electricity." We will learn all that took place on that western edge where
every shining object sets, and build from it a train for our thoughts.
Following this, we will turn back to the future where the sun rises in order
to welcome the newcomers, demonstrating and observing from afar the
morning of happiness. We will board the train of progress and the ship of
labor and endeavor, both of which attract Divine help, and with lamps in
our hands, enter that part of time that has a dark beginning but a bright
future. In the end, we will shake hands with future generations and congratulate them on their happiness.

This small illustration contains a beautiful scene; in the following
pages it will present itself to you through words. In the ground marked out
here the trees of the future chapters of this book will grow.

O brothers and sisters! Now in order to hold your hand and take you to
the treasury of truth, I will deal with some matters, trying to remove the

phantasms before your eyes that prevent you from seeing clearly. These phantasms veil your eyes and frighten you. Even if they do not completely prevent you from seeing, they cause light to appear as fire and pearls as pebbles. Avoid these phantasms. The main source of your suspicions and misconceptions are some particular matters, many of which are concerned with the earth. These are the Prophetic Tradition which says that the earth stands on an ox and a fish, and the matters such as the nature of Mount Qaf, the barrier of Dhu'l-Qarnayn (Qur'an, 18: 93–96), the Qur'anic description of mountains as masts (78:7), the statement that Hell is located under the earth, and other issues mentioned in the following Qur'anic statements:

> He sends down hail out of snow-laden mountains from the sky (24:43);
>
> And the sun runs the course appointed for it for a term to its resting place for its stability (36:38);
>
> He has spread out the earth (in egg-shape for habitability) (79:30);
>
> And the earth—how it has been spread out? (88:20)

I will explain the truth of these matters so that the enemies of the Religion can no longer exploit them against the Religion, and so that the eyes of its friends will be opened.

First Matter

It is known and admitted by fair minds that the verifying Muslim scholars explicitly or implicitly agree that the earth is spherical. If you still have doubts, you can consult Sharhu'l-Maqasid and Sharhu'l-Mawaqif, books in which the great Muslim theologians of the Middle Ages, Sa'd al-Din al-Taftazani[24] and Sayyid Sharif al-Jurjani,[25] hold the earth in their hands like a ball and make observations about it.

---

[24] Sharh al-Maqasid, 'Alam al-Kutub, Beirut, 1998, 3:177–189. Sa'd al-Din al-Taftazani (d., 1390): A famous scholar of logic, rhetoric, grammar, theology, and jurisprudence of Samarqand during the rule of Timur. His Sharh al-'Aqaid al-Nasafiyya ("An Exposition of the Book of Creed by al-Nasafi") is among the basic works of the Muslim theology. (Trans.)

[25] Sharh al-Mawaqif, Dar al-Kutub al-'Ilmiyya, Beirut, 7:145–147. Sayyid Sharif al-Jurjani (d., 1413): One of the leading theologians of the fifteenth century. He visited Istanbul in 1374, and upon his return, in 1377, he was given a teaching appointment in Shiraz. Sharh al-Mawaqif is his most famous work. (Trans.)

If you are searching for yet another source, you can examine the voluminous commentary on the Qur'an by Imam Fakhr al-Din al-Razi,[26] *Mafatih al-Ghayb*, and pay heed to what that illustrious Imam tells you.

If you are still not content with his explanations and cannot fit the earth into its spherical shape, then apply to Ibrahim Haqqi of Erzurum.[27] You can also visit Imam al-Ghazali and ask him if there is any disagreement among the Muslim scholars about the spherical shape of the earth. He will certainly say to you, "If you do not accept its spherical shape, it is wrong and reprehensible." For he has sent this judgment to us from his time: "Whoever denies the undeniable fact that the earth is spherical on the pretext of preserving the Religion commits a horrible crime against the Religion. For this is not faithfulness, it is betrayal."[28]

If you do not know how to read or write and therefore you cannot read them, give ear to Husayn al-Jisri,[29] a contemporary scholar. He threatens with a loud voice those who deny the spherical shape of the earth, and declares with the power of truth, "Whoever denies that the earth is spherical with the excuse of preserving the Religion and claims that his denial is based on the Religion, they are a foolish friend, and do more harm to the Religion than a great enemy."[30]

---

[26] *Mafatih al-Ghayb*, Dar al-Kutub al-'Ilmiyya, Beirut, 2003, 31:48. Muhammad ibn 'Umar Fakhr al-Dīn al-Razi, (d., 1210): One of the most famous commentators of the Qur'an and the most outstanding scholars of his time who was well versed in both religious and rational sciences. *Mafatih al-Ghayb* is the name of his monumental commentary on the Qur'an. (Trans.)

[27] Ibrahim Haqqi of Erzurum (1703–1780) was one of the most outstanding figures in the O - toman Turkey of the eighteenth century. He lived in Erzurum and Siirt in Eastern Turkey. He was a prolific, encyclopedic Sufi guide and writer, who wrote on many subjects such as theology, morality, mathematics, astronomy, and medicine. His *Ma'rifatname* ("Book of Knowledge") is very famous and still being widely read. In the third volume of this book, Ibrahim Haqqi of Erzurum discusses the spherical shape of the earth and celestial bodies at length. (Trans.)

[28] *Tahafut al-Falasifa*, ("The Incoherence of the Philosophers"), Dar al-Ma'arif, Cairo 1972, p. 80.

[29] Husayn al-Jisri (1845–1909) was born and mainly lived in Lebanon. He was well versed in Islamic sciences, and had an interest in natural sciences. He founded a *madrasa* where both kinds of sciences were taught. His thoughts greatly resembled those of Said Nursi about both religious and contemporary issues. (Trans.)

[30] *Risale-i Hamidiya* (Turkish trans.,) Bahar Yayınları, Istanbul, 1980, 365–367.

If the truth, which has long slept, does not awaken within you with this loud voice, and your heart does not open, take scholars such as Ibn Humam[31] and Fakhr al-Islam[32] by the hand, and go to Imam al-Shafi'i.[33] Ask him: "The Shari'a orders the Prayer at five fixed times. But in the world there are people in whose country there is sometimes no time for the Late Evening or Night Prayer. There are people in other countries where the sun does not rise for many consecutive days, or does not set during other consecutive days. How do they fast?" Ask him again, "Turning towards the Ka'ba is compulsory during the Prayer. But we can turn toward it only while standing or sitting. How can we turn toward the Ka'ba in other acts of the Prayer such as during bowing and prostration?"

Be sure that Imam al-Shafi'i will explain the first and second matters with the spherical shapes of the latitudes and the elliptical shapes of the longitudes.[34] He will speak in such a convincing manner, demonstrating the rational proofs that are in his hands. He will say, concerning the matter of turning toward the Ka'ba during all the acts of the Prayer, "The direction which we take during the Prayer is a perpendicular line of light that ties the heavens to the Supreme Divine Throne and penetrates through the

---

31   Kamal al-Din Muhammad ibn Abd al-Wahid ibn Humam al-Sivasi al-Iskandari (1388–1457) was one of the leading Muslim scholars. He belonged to a family which emigrated from Sivas in Turkey to Iskandariya (Alexandria) in Egypt. He was famous both as a jurist (*faqih*) and traditionist (*muhaddith*). Among his works is *Fath al-Qadir*, in which he expands on *al-Hidaya*, one of the most famous works on Hanafi *fiqh* by Imam Burhan al-Din Abu al-Hasan al-Marginani (1117–1196), with long explanatory notes. (Trans.)

32   Fakhr al-Islam Abu'l-Hasan 'Ali ibn Muhammad al-Pazdawi (1009–1089) was one of the most prominent legal theorists or methodologists (*usuliyyun*) in the Hanafi School of *Fiqh*. He lived in Transoxania. *Usul al-Din* ("The Fundamentals of the Religion") is his most famous work. (Trans.)

33   Imam al-Shafi'i, Muhammad ibn Idris (d. 820): Founded the Shafi'i School of Law. He was well versed in Islamic jurisprudence, Hadith language, and poetry. He wrote *Al-Umm* ("The Foundation"), *al-Risalah* ("A Book of Methodology"), and *Ahkam al-Qur'an* ("Judgments of the Qur'an"). (Trans.)

34   That is, the earth is egg-shaped, spherical from east to west and elliptical from north to south. In the polar or similar regions, where days and nights are much longer than our normal days and nights or the time of a Prayer does not occur, signs of morning and evening do appear with unfailing regularity and the people know them. People living there can also make an estimate of time considering the times of the Prayers in other regions where every day is twenty-four hours, and fast or perform the Prayers. (Trans.)

strata of the earth down to its center."[35] If the veil over your eyes is removed, the rays of your sight will bring together all the acts of the Prayer in the direction we turn to during Prayer.

O brothers and sisters! I see that you are not sure of your claims against the Religion; you cannot convince your conscience, and your whims can only find room for themselves in your imagination. So abandon your prejudices, and if the earth cannot find room in your hearts, which are closed to the truth but open to whims and illusions, widen your view. Ask the inhabitants of this house, the earth, for they know their own house. They will tell you, "The earth, which is our cradle and mount in this vast space, is not mad, moving in a disorderly way; it is bound by the same laws of God as the other celestial bodies, it cannot infringe them by acting on its own. (They are spherical, as are all other planetary bodies.)" They will also spread out maps as another proof of the earth's spherical shape.[36]

AN INDICATION

The Divine laws of the creation and operation of the universe have stipulated that this guesthouse—the earth, which revolves in ecstasy like a Mevlevi dervish—stand in the line of the planets and obeys the sun. For together with its friend—the heavens—they have told God, "We have come in willing obedience" (41: 11).[37] Obedience and worship are better when done in congregation. In short, the Creator of the universe has created the earth in the way that He has willed. He has not created it according to the wishes of anybody, nor has He allowed the reason of any one person to be the engineer for it.

---

[35] That is, he refers to the spherical shape of the earth and circular appearance of the hea - ens, which seem to be joining the earth on the horizons. (Trans.)

[36] Even on maps of the earth, which are two-dimensional, the parts of the earth do not a - pear to be of size proportionate to their actual size. The parts from which makers of maps see the earth in drawing them appear to be larger, while the other parts, smaller. If we see the earth from the Equator in drawing a map, the central parts will appear to be considerably larger proportionate to their actual size, while the parts lying towards the north and south will appear to be smaller and smaller towards the poles. (Trans.)

[37] The Qur'an says, And He directed (His Knowledge, Will, Power, and Favor) to the heaven when it was as a cloud (of gases) and ordered it and the earth, "Come both of you, willingly or unwillingly!" They said: "We have come in willing obedience." (41:11) (Trans.)

A REMINDER

One of the attitudes that indicate a weakness of belief and a tendency to sophism is the foolish saying, "This is opposed to the Religion, even though it is an established fact." Anyone who deems it probable that something which has been uncontrovertibly established can be opposed to the Religion, which is itself an embodiment of pure truth and accommodates every truth, has either sophistry in their minds or cherishes doubts which give rise to rebellion in their hearts, or is a new adherent to the Religion and desires to be free to criticize it according to their own misguided views.

Second Matter

It is doubtful whether the narration that *the earth rests on the ox and fish* is attributed with certainty to the Prophet, upon him be peace and blessings. For this reason, we are not religiously obliged to accept it as a Prophetic Tradition. Even if it is a Prophetic Tradition, it is not clear that the ox and the fish mentioned in it were used literally. You can consult the Fifth and Eleventh Premises. You will see how fancies distract literalists from the truth.

This Tradition has three significant interpretations, all of which are correct:

The first: The bearers of the Divine Throne are sometimes called the Ox, the Vulture, the Man, or some other title. These are in fact angels. Therefore the ox and fish mentioned in the Tradition in question could be referring to these angels. Otherwise, the placing of the Divine Throne and the earth on the back of an ox, an animal which is not self-sufficient, is opposed to the order of the universe. In addition, we learn from the Shari'a: There is an angel appointed for every species of existence; this angel manages the affairs of that species. The angel is called by the name of the species for which it is responsible and appears with its form in the world of the angels. There is a Prophetic Tradition: "The sun goes up before the Divine Throne every evening, prostrates itself, and is given permission to return."[38] The angel responsible for the sun is called "the Sun," and is in the shape of the sun. So, the sun that the Prophetic Tradition mentions as going up

---

[38] Al-Bukhari, *al-Jami' al-Sahih*, "Tafsir Sura Ya-Sin" 1; " 39; Muslim, *al-Jami' al-Sahih*, "Iman" 250.

before the Divine Throne is in fact this angel. The philosophers who study theology mention a different living and speaking spiritual entity that comes to the aid of every species of creation and asks God for help in the name of that species. In the Shari'a these entities are called the Angel of the Mountains, the Angel of the Seas, the Angel of the Rain, and so on. But they have no creative effect on anything or on any event. The One Who creates everything and every event without any interference, help, or contribution from anything else, is God alone.

No one but God has a part in creation. However, in order that people should not see the Divine Hand of Power involved in some "low" or apparently distressing things and events, God employs apparent means and causes as a veil before His Dignity and Grandeur. But in the realm of pure truths and spirituality, which is what the creed is essentially concerned with or aims at, everything exists in its transcendental beauty and purity. The Divine Power works here without employing any veils. This is what the All-Glorious, the All-Knowing destines and decrees.

The Tradition in question has another meaning. The ox is the most important animal for agriculture. Fish are the basic livelihood for many people, particularly those living in coastal regions. If one asks us what keeps a state standing, we might answer, "The state depends on the pen and sword." If we are asked what makes a civilization endure, we might answer, "It endures by science, skills, and economy." Or if they ask what humanity subsists by, we might answer, "It subsists by knowledge and labor." The Prophet, who is the pride of creation, upon him be peace and blessings, could well have meant this when he said, "The earth stands on the ox and fish." If the one who asked him what the earth stood on was unable to understand a scientific answer, he would have been given the answer most appropriate to his level of understanding. That is, our Prophet, upon him be peace and blessings, may have been answering this person figuratively—meaning that the majority of people lived either by farming and agriculture, for which oxen were indispensable, or by fishing. Since a considerable portion of the population lived by the seashore and their basic livelihood was fish, their world "stands on" fish. It is like the saying of the Arabs, "The whole of game is in the belly of the wild ass." Since wild asses were the primary target of some Arab hunters, they would say that to mean that one who hunted a wild ass did not need to pursue other game.

The answer of the Pride of Creation, upon him be peace and blessings, who always spoke the truth even when joking, is highly significant. He gave the answer that was necessary and appropriate so that the person who asked the question could understand. It is a rule of rhetoric that one who asks sometimes receives an answer that they do not expect. The answer should be couched in such a way that it will be useful to and understandable by the person asking. It must also meet a need and must not give rise to misunderstandings or further doubts or confusion. When some people asked the Prophet, upon him be peace and blessings, about the new moons, God Almighty answered in the Qur'an, *They ask you about the new moons. Say: "They are appointed times (markers) for the people (to determine time periods) and for the Pilgrimage."* (2: 189)

The Tradition under discussion has a third important meaning. Taurus (the ox) and Pisces (the fish) are two astrological signs of the zodiac. Even though these signs are imaginary, the Divine laws that operate in the universe, including the law of gravity, are focused on them. Thus, saying that the earth stands on these signs of the zodiac indicates a scientific reality. Such an expression, used at a time when the science of the time thought that these signs actually existed in the sky, gains greater importance in the present, because astronomy now considers that they are related to the annual orbit of the earth.

It is reported that the Prophet was twice asked about the location of the earth. In one of his answers, he said that it was on a fish. When asked the second time, he said that it was on an ox. When he said that the earth was on a fish, the rays or threads of the law of gravitation, which prevails throughout the heavens, were focused and intersected on the sign of Pisces, and the earth, which was leaving the sign of Aquarius, held fast to this law and, for the appointed duration, hung on a branch of the Tree of Creation like a fruit, or alighted like a bird. Continuing to orbit, the earth progressed to the sign of Taurus, and thus, the Prophet, upon him be peace and blessings, said that the earth was on an ox.

With that reality in mind, we can say that taking the Tradition literally, as some dreamers do, only means attributing absurdity to the eternal Divine Wisdom, and destroying the miraculous order of the universe, which bears witness to the existence and Oneness of the Creator.

Third Matter

This is concerned with Mount Qaf.

AN INDICATION

Knowing and affirming the existence of something is different from knowing its nature and identity. We should distinguish these two points from each other, as there are many things humans can imagine as not existing, although their existence is evident. You can consult the Seventh Premise. Also, there are many texts on which numerous personal views have been presented concerning their meaning. You can consult the Eleventh Premise.

A REMINDER

Taking into consideration these two points, we can examine the matter of Mount Qaf. The only indication of Qaf in the Qur'an and the sound Prophetic Traditions is the verse (50:1): *Qaf. By the Qur'an most sublime.* The original referent of the *Qaf* mentioned in this verse is a letter of the Arabic alphabet. Its location is not in the east of the world but in the part of the mouth uttering the sound of that consonant. So, this has nothing to do with Mount Qaf. Another argument for *Qaf* not being an allusion to Mount Qaf is that al-Qarafi,[39] a great scholar of the Shari'a, decisively rejects the existence of such a mountain. You can consult the Fourth Premise with regard to what is reported from Ibn 'Abbas concerning the existence of a mountain called Qaf. Whatever Ibn 'Abbas said is not necessarily a report from the Prophet, upon him be peace and blessings. Nor are we obliged to regard whatever he quoted from others as being true, as we know that during his youth, Ibn 'Abbas took help from Israelite sources in order to clarify certain things (not otherwise clear to him).

If you ask about certain descriptions of Mount Qaf by some Sufi scholars, I answer as follows:

---

[39] Shihab al-Din Abu'l-'Abbas Ahmad ibn Idris al-Qarafi (?–1285) lived in Egypt. Well-versed in both jurisprudence (*fiqh*) and theology (*kalam*), he was one of the most outstanding scholars in the Maliki School of *Fiqh*. He also wrote on optics. *Kitabu'l-Istibsar fima Tudrikuhu'l-Absar* ("The Book of Insight into What Eyes Comprehend") is his book on optics. (Trans.)

The world of symbols or imaginal or "ideal" forms is the place in which Sufis travel. They are removed from their bodies as we are removed from our clothes; thus, they are able to make spiritual journeys in this world of wonders. *Qaf* is observed in this world as they describe it. Just as the sky is reflected in a mirror with its stars, a little thing in our world of corporeality—a mental or spiritual reality embodied—becomes like a tall tree in the world of imaginal forms. We should not confuse the realities of these two worlds with one another. One who understands the real meaning of Muhyi al-Din ibn al-'Arabi's[40] words will confirm this. The common people imagine *Qaf* to be a range of mountains surrounding the earth that comprises many great peaks, each millions of miles distant from the other. They touch the edge of the sky. People make descriptions as far-fetched as their imagination can travel. If you would like to see the value of their imaginings, you can use the Third Premise as a lamp, and enter this darkness with it.

If you ask about my personal view on this matter: I am convinced that *Qaf* exists but I cannot say anything about what it is. If I come across a sound, reliably narrated Prophetic Tradition about the nature of it, I will believe that what the Prophet meant by it is certainly true, and try to understand what he meant, ignoring the fancies people have developed. For it sometimes happens that we infer meanings from a saying other than what its speaker really meant.

The *Qaf* described as mountain ranges might be the Himalayas, including the second highest mountain range of Kangchenjunga (8,586 m) (and K2 or Dapsang, Kechu or Ketu), which used to separate the civilized and uncivilized peoples in the past. Some say that many of the mountains in the Old World spread out from this range. So it may be thought that the idea that *Qaf* is a mountain range surrounding the whole world originates from the fact that the Himalayas were the "mother" of many mountain ranges.

Another approach to *Qaf* may be that the world of symbols or imaginal or "ideal" forms is an intermediate realm between the corporeal and

---

40 Muhyi al-Din ibn al-'Arabi (1165–1240): One of the greatest and most famous Sufi masters. His doctrine of the Transcendental Unity of Existence, which most have mistaken for monism and pantheism, made him the target of unending polemics. He wrote many books, the most famous of which are *Fusus al-Hikam* and *al-Futuhat al-Makkiyyah*. (Trans.)

unseen worlds. The world of symbols or imaginal forms resembles the corporeal world in the shapes and the unseen world in the meanings it contains. Whoever so desires can enter this world through the window of sound spiritual discovery or true dreams or with the power of the imagination. There is much evidence for the existence of that world; the meanings from our world taking on different forms there. So the *Qaf* which is in this world may be the seed of the extraordinary *Qaf* that exists in that world.

The dominion of God is infinite, and cannot be restricted to our tiny sphere. Thus, *Qaf* can have many extraordinary aspects. Although our sphere does not include a distance of millions of miles, it is not unreasonable to think that *Qaf* is something transparent and invisible or that it touches the edge of the sky, which is a tightened or straightened wave.

As another way of explanation: what is there to preclude *Qaf* being a great range of mountains stretching along the horizon? The Arabic root for the word horizon is *ufq*, and it may have been from this root that *Qaf* originated. For wherever we look, we see a surrounding circle, comprised of a series of concentric circles. We cannot see beyond the horizon, and the duty of going beyond falls to the power of imagination. The power of imagination sees that there is a range of mountains along the horizon that encircles the world and touches the sky. Since the earth and horizon are circular, even if this range extends millions of miles, it is seen to be a single, connected range of mountains.

Fourth Matter

This is the barrier built by Dhu'l-Qarnayn (The Qur'an, 18:92–98).

As stated before, knowing and affirming the existence of something is different from knowing its nature and identity. In addition, in any piece of writing, article or book, there may be many judgments. Some of these judgments are explicit, established, and of primary importance, while others are putative or ambiguous. If a knowledgeable one is asked about a matter discussed in a book written long before and which has been partially changed over time, the answer will take either or both of the two forms. Either, it will be in agreement with the aim and terms of the questioner's question, or it will be of the kind that gives rise to further inter-

pretative effort by the questioner. So, in addition to being in agreement
with the reality and convincing the questioner (that his question in the
terms asked has been answered), a proper answer may also solve other
aspects of the problem that the questioner had not anticipated when asking the question. Even if the answer may not always exactly conform to
the aim of the questioner in asking his question in the way he did, by
applying the answer to his knowledge about the matter, he in fact received
the right answer. In addition, if the person answering takes into consideration the conditions in which the question is asked, the answer will contribute to many other purposes by virtue of the core of the vitality in it.
The answers in the Qur'an are of this kind.

    We should distinguish between the explicit judgments to be found in
any Qur'anic statements and those that are not explicit, without forgetting
that it is obligatory to believe in the explicit ones. The explicit points in
the Qur'an's answer to the question about Dhu'l-Qarnayn cannot be
denied. According to this answer (18:83–98), Dhu'l-Qarnayn was a person
favored with God's confirmation and help. By God's leave and guidance,
he built a barrier between two mountains in order to prevent the attacks
and corruption of some savages—Gog and Magog are the names given to
the two "tribes" that were engaged in corruption and disorder. When the
Divine order comes, the barrier will be destroyed. These, and some other
explicit truths that exist in the Qur'an's account of Dhu'l-Qarnayn, must
certainly be considered as being confirmed. Denial of any of them means
unbelief. However, as for the detail of what is narrated and meanings that
it is possible to infer—the Qur'an is not clear about them. According to
the rule that an expression employed to convey a general meaning does
not necessarily constitute an argument or proof for some particular meaning incidental to that general meaning or alluded to or required by it, and
the rule that whatever a statement states clearly with respect to its underlying and essential meaning is sufficient for it, it may be said that the
Qur'an here does not necessarily indicate anything of detail. But since it
does not categorically reject it, we can study and comment on it.

    This means that all the interpretations, expositions, and analyses, other
than the explicit meaning and the clear, apparent truth established by the
explicit meaning, are only putative suggestions. They require corroboration
by other indications. Interpreters can reason about them. They can be given

different meanings. The differences of opinion among verifying scholars concerning them shows that the inferences and connotations, other than the evident, basic meanings are putative. But unfortunately, some people attempted to arrive at different, conflicting conclusions from the verses, as if the answer should come exactly in accordance with the purpose of the questioner; they did not consider the error in or the hidden intent behind asking the question or behind inferring meanings from the verses that had arisen according to the sources that had provoked the questioner. They added into the essential meaning their personal interpretations and certain persons or events that they regarded as fitting into the Qur'anic account. Even that was not enough; they went on to present these as if they were the essential, evident meaning. The literalists accepted such interpretations and inferences as being part of the essential meaning, while the verifying scholars considered them as harmless stories, and did not criticize them. However, acceptance of certain interpretations and inferences based on or borrowed from the present altered versions of the Bible is contrary to the creed of Islam and the sinlessness of the Prophets. The stories narrated in the Bible concerning Prophets such as Lot and David, upon them be peace, bear witness to what I say.

Since deductive reasoning is permitted in the secondary or explanatory matters where the Qur'an and the sound Prophetic Tradition are silent, and commenting while relying on God's help, is permissible, I say: What the Qur'an and our Prophet meant by Dhu'l-Qarnayn, Gog and Magog, and the barrier which Dhu'l-Qarnayn built is absolutely true, and it is obligatory to believe in these. For believing in whatever the Qur'an and our Prophet said and meant is one of the fundamentals of the Religion. However, when what the Qur'an and the Prophet say is not clear, we are allowed to make comments. So, concerning the matters under discussion, I say the following:

I do not agree with those who claim that Dhu'l-Qarnayn was Alexander the Great. First of all, the name does not fit this. Some interpreters of the Qur'an assert that he was a king, while according to some, he was an angel, others maintain that he was a Prophet, and there are some who think that he was a saint. What is certain in the Qur'an is that Dhu'l-Qarnayn was one who was confirmed and strengthened by God and who caused a barrier to be built between certain civilized and uncivilized peoples. There are also differences of view about the barrier. Some interpreters say that it was the Great Wall of China. Some others look for it between some mountains, and still others hold that it was a barrier that disappeared over time. Wherever and whatever it was or is, what is certain is that it was a great barrier for repelling the attacks of some savage, plundering tribes.

As for the tribes of Gog and Magog, there are different views among the interpreters. According to some interpreters, they were two tribes that were descendents of Noah's son Yafas, while some others opine that they were some Mongolian and Manchurian tribes, or two tribes that were living in north-eastern Asia. There are still some who hold the view that they were a great host who reduced the world to chaos, while some others maintain that they are some creatures among God's human and non-human beings who live on or under the surface of the earth and who will throw the world into great chaos before the Last Day. Despite such different views, all interpreters are agreed that Gog and Magog are two savage tribes who signal the end of the civilized world.

There are several opinions about how the barrier came or comes to an end. According to some, it will be destroyed before the end of time, while others say that the signs of its being destroyed have already appeared, and it will be fully demolished in the future. There are still others who are of the opinion that it was destroyed long ago. The common point on which all are agreed is that the destruction of the barrier means a grey hair in the beard of the earth and signals the old age of humankind.

When you consider all these explanations, it is possible to conclude that the Great Wall of China may have a share in the meaning or identity of the barrier. Extending for thousands of kilometers, this Wall is one of the Seven Wonders of the World, and, at least at the beginning or during some period of its construction, it must have been built by one confirmed and strengthened by God. At the time it was built to protect the civilized peoples of the world from the destructive power of the savages. The destruction of the barrier is one of the signs of the final destruction of the world. Its complete disappearance is something different. The Prophet held up his two fingers side by side and declared, "I and the end of the world are like these two fingers,"[41] meaning that he was the last of the Prophets, and was one of the

---

41   Al-Bukhari, al-Jami' al-Sahih, "Riqaq" 39; Muslim, al-Jami' al-Sahih, "Fitan" 132–135; al-Tirmidhi, Sunan, "Fitan" 39.

signs of the end of the world. So, why should not the destruction of the barrier after the Age of Happiness—the Age of the Prophet—be a sign that the end of time is nigh? The destruction of the barrier suggests a wrinkle on the face of the earth, signaling its old age. There may be a time period between the destruction of the barrier and the final destruction of the world or Doomsday in the lifetime of the world that is like the time between the late afternoon and the evening; that time period may last hundreds or even thousands of years. Likewise, the turmoil and destruction that is to be caused by Gog and Magog could be the fever of humankind in its old age.

The comment made at the beginning of the Twelfth Premise concerning the narrative and the lesson will open a door for you. It is as follows:

The Qur'an mentions historical events to give certain, important lessons, and picks certain points out of these events which are like the nuclei of life and which serve one or some of its main purposes. Although the fire and light of a narrative and the lesson it gives do not exist side by side (that is, the lesson is not mentioned along with the narrative but is inferred from it,) the style may show them to be close friends standing side by side, and the mind may see them to be so. But since an event is narrated to teach a lesson, detail is not important. We should take the lesson without considering the detail. Furthermore, when you consult the Tenth Premise, you will see that one metaphor opens a door onto another. The sentence, *He (Dhu'l-Qarnayn) saw it (the sun) setting in a spring of hot and black, muddy water* (18: 86), rejects the literalists.

It should be remembered that the key of many Divine truths and proofs manifested through the language of Arabic is rhetorical eloquence founded upon the concise, figurative or metaphorical styles. The key to understanding them is not the speculations people make concerning the statements of Divine Speech. If you like, consult the Conclusion of the Tenth Premise, from which you can extract the nectar. It is also possible that the barrier, the exact identity and location of which are unknown to us, may be somewhere in the world, and will survive until the destruction of the world on Doomsday.

AN INDICATION

A house is not built for endurance, with no use at all. A house exists because it should be inhabited, but it usually outlives its dwellers. Similarly, a fort does not exist for a certain period of time without any use; it exists because people should take shelter in it, but it usually endures more than those who take shelter in it. There are many buildings which were built for habitation or to take shelter in, but which continue to exist empty and with no purpose. (So, although Dhu'l-Qarnayn built the barrier against the attacks of savage peoples, this does not require its destruction when its use has ended. It is possible that it will survive until the destruction of the world.) Unawareness of or heedlessness to this reality has given rise to many fancies and misunderstandings.

A REMINDER

The reason why I have gone into this lengthy explanation concerning Dhu'l-Qarnayn and certain relevant matters is to illustrate the need to distinguish the exact meaning of a statement from its interpretations, something certain from something conjectural, the existence of something from its nature, a judgment (in the source texts themselves) from the explanations of others, the essential meaning of a statement from the points relating to that meaning, and the need to consider an occurrence with an eye to the likelihood of its occurring.

Fifth Matter

Hell is under the earth. The Ahl al-Sunnah wa-l-Jama'a, namely the Sunni majority among the Muslims, are not certain about its exact location. However, they generally accept that Hell is under the earth. Based on this, I would say that like other spheres, the earth is one of the fruits of the huge tree of creation, which resembles the Tuba tree in Paradise. Under the fruit are all the branches of the tree. God's dominion is infinite, and the tree of creation has extended its branches throughout. So, Hell is located on one of those branches. It is not important whether it lies under the earth contiguously with or at a distance from the earth. According to modern science, fire, in different forms, is diffuse throughout a great part of the universe. This indicates that Hell, the source of fire which will accompany humankind along its way to eternity, will one day tear away its veil, call humankind to be ready to meet it, and be brought forth with all its dread. I would like to draw your attention to the following point:

What is meant by "under the earth" is the inner part of the earth, its core. This means that the earth holds within it the seed of the Zaqqum tree of Hell. A day will come when this seed germinates and blossoms. The earth, which moves through space, will give birth from this seed to such a thing that even if all of Hell may not be contained within it, some part of Hell is there and that part will grow into Hell after Doomsday, and this will be the abode of the rebellious.

Even if Hell cannot now be reached to be observed, mathematics and geology will take one there. For every 33 meters that one descends towards the earth's core the heat increases by 1°C. Thus, as the radius of the earth is 6,000 kilometers, the core is thought to have a temperature of nearly 200,000 °C. This heat, two hundred times more intense that the heat on the surface of the earth, which can reach 1,000 °C at the most, is in agreement with the Prophetic Tradition that states, "The heat of Hell is two hundred times more intense than our heat."[42] In addition, some part of Hell burns with coldness. There is a degree of fire called *nar-i bayda* (white fire). It does not emit heat around it; rather, it absorbs heat, and makes the air around cold.

A REMINDER

It should be borne in mind that the world of eternity cannot be measured on the scales of this world. If you are patient, you will be familiar with the Hereafter at the end of the Third Part of this book.

AN INDICATION

From the testimony of the perfect order of the universe, which is borne out by sciences; the guidance of inductive reasoning (that is, the instances of death and revival observed in individuals and species signaling the final universal death and revival); the indication of human essence; the hint of the limitlessness of human ambitions; the reminder of numerous instances of the Resurrection observed every day and every year; the fact that there is nothing useless in creation; the enlightenment of the reality that every-

---

[42] For similar Traditions, see, al-Bukhari, *Ibid*, "Bad'ul-Khalq" 10; Muslim, *Ibid*, "Janna" 29; al-Tirmidhi, *Sunan*, "Jahannam" 7.

thing is created for a certain purpose; the demonstration of infinite Divine Mercy; and most importantly of all, the decisive declarations of the Prophet, who always spoke the truth; and the guidance of the miraculous Qur'an— from all these (scientific, rational, and religious) proofs there are eight doors and two windows that open on the view of reason from the eternal happiness that is to be experienced in Paradise.

Sixth Matter

It is an established fact that the most distinguishing feature of the revealed Qur'an is that it is a miracle. Its miraculousness or inimitability primarily lies in the matchless degree of its eloquence. Eloquence is founded upon certain elements of style, including in particular metaphors, allegories, and other figures of speech. One who does not look at the Qur'an through the binoculars of these elements cannot see its merits. For God, Who has made all knowledge flow in the Qur'an through the channels of the style of the Arabic language, considers the levels of emotions, sensations, and understanding of human beings. This being so, interpreters of the Qur'an must pay full respect to the Qur'an and, therefore, should not attempt to interpret it based on things that do not bear the stamp of eloquence. For it has been established as one of the clearest and brightest truths that just as the meanings or content of the Qur'an is true throughout, it also has perfectly eloquent styles and wording, which are the form or embodiment of meaning. For this reason, whoever does not base their thoughts on this source when interpreting will become among "the frauds who deceive in weighing and measuring" with respect to paying the Qur'an its due. I will mention a few significant examples:

The first: We have made mountains as masts (78: 7). (God knows best.) The figurative style in the verse gives the impression that the earth is a ship sailing in the ocean of space.[43] It has been made stable by the mountains, which are its masts, and is thus balanced in the air. So, the mountains are the masts of that ship.

Secondly, the tremors in the belly of the earth are controlled through the mountains. The mountains are like the pores of the earth. When there

---

[43] Since the space is full of ether, a pervasive gas like fluid, Said Nursi uses the term, "the ocean of space." (Trans.)

is unrest in the belly, the earth breathes in and out through the mountains and its anger stops. This means that the calmness and silence of the earth are maintained through the mountains.

Thirdly, the pillar of the improvement of the earth is humanity, and the pillar of human life is the preservation of air, water, and soil, which are the sources of life. It is the mountains which secure this. For in addition to being reservoirs where the water is kept, the mountains also serve to filter air and preserve its freshness. As they balance heat and cold by absorbing harmful gases mixed with air, they enable its purification. In addition, they are the sources of soil, and also preserve the soil from the onslaughts of seas and marshes.

Fourthly, this simile for the earth gives the idea that if a person flies above in the balloon of imagination and looks down on the ranges of mountains, they can imagine the soil to be the tents of nomads and the mountains to be their poles. If from the point where you have ascended you look through the binoculars of wisdom and science down at the earth, the cradle of humanity, and the sky, the raised dome, and imagine the sky, limited by the horizon formed along the ranges of mountains, to be the dome of a tent set up on the earth and fastened with the masts of mountains, no one will find fault with you.

In the section "A Reminder" to be included in the Eighth Matter, some other examples will be given.

Seventh Matter

In order to confuse minds and cast doubt on the authenticity of the Qur'an some people, only taking into consideration the literal meaning, have put forward some objections to the following:

> He (Dhu'l-Qarnayn) saw it setting in a spring of hot and black, muddy water (18:86).

> And the earth, We have spread it out like a couch (51:48).

> And the earth, how it has been spread out (88:20).

> And after that He has spread out the earth in egg-shape (79:30).

In fact, there is no need to answer such objections. Illustrious interpreters of the Qur'an have brought to light the gems contained in such expressions. Without leaving any need for further explanation, they have taught us what we should know.

> Those who lived in earlier times wept and caused me also to weep.
> Alas! Are there any who will relent because of my weeping?

It is futile to attempt to teach what is already known, especially if the thing that is known is observable. It must therefore contain some peculiar and remarkable points so that it may not be futile to teach or state it. So, if it had been said: see how the earth was made a couch for living beings despite its spherical shape and how it has been protected against the rising of the seas; how, despite its supposed stability, the sun runs its course to serve us in procuring our livelihood; how the sun, which is millions of miles away from us, sets in "a spring of hot and black, muddy water," then the verses mentioned would have had no points worthy of attention. The points (that some so-called modernists make a target of criticism) are in fact aspects of eloquence.

Eighth Matter

AN INDICATION

One of the factors, rather, the primary factor, which puts literalists in danger is that they take a possibility for a fact. For example, they say, "The Divine Power can do that. Moreover, it is more befitting, according to reason, for His Grandeur to do so. So, this must be so." This is sheer stupidity. O poor ones! Has your reason developed to the point where it can measure and engineer the universe? How can you, with your restricted reason, comprehend the universal system with all its parts and features and perceive its overall beauty? These are the kind of people who, if there were a golden nose half a meter long, would see it as more beautiful and fitting for people because, devoid of the holistic approach, they restrict their views to the object alone.

Another disastrous thing which causes their bewilderment is their false supposition that something that they suppose to occur is opposed to the certainty of knowledge. Because of this, they feel doubts about matters that are observably clear; they resemble sophists and (scientific) agnostics. According to their way of thought, we should doubt the existence of, for example, Lake Van or Mount Süphan, because according to them, their actual existence does not negate their supposed non-existence. They also see it as possible for Lake Van to change into a lake of molasses and for Mount Süphan to become a heap of honey covered with sugar. Again, since according to those friends and people like them, that sea and mountain do not consent to the earth being spherical and have set out on a journey, it is possible for them to stumble and fall into an ocean. For this reason, we cannot confirm that they remain in their places. O poor fellows! There can be no room for doubt about the things we perceive with our five external senses. If you deny an observed fact, I will, instead of giving you advice, offer my condolences for your "death." For the clearest knowledge everybody possesses has died and sophistry has been revived in you.

The third disaster, which bewilders literalists, is that they confuse something that is possible in their imagination with its being rationally possible. But something that is possible in the imagination is not founded upon anything substantial, and causes doubts about even the most plain truths, leading to questions and sayings such as, "Why should it not be so?", "It may well become so!" This arises from a lack of reasoning, a weakness in the heart, a sickness in the mind, and the supposition that there is no evidence for any truth. Contrary to this, rational possibilities or something being rationally or reasonably possible means feeling doubt about a matter for both the existence and non-existence of which there is no substantial evidence. Whimsical or fanciful possibilities cause one to say, "It is possible that this thing is not as it is shown to be by that fact. For reason is unable to comprehend everything. Furthermore, our reason considers that it may be so."

No! It is not your reason, but your whims and imagination that lead to you to think something may be as you claim. Reason follows evidence. It is true that reason cannot weigh everything, but it can easily weigh material existence, including in particular the things that cannot escape the eyes, no matter how small they are. We are not responsible for those things that reason cannot evaluate.

A REMINDER

Those whom I mention or criticize as literalists or the ones who restrict themselves to the external are people who are either the enemies of Islam looking at it from afar with a superficial view, unable to perceive its beauty, or its ignorant friends who do it harm while trying to help.

The fourth disaster is precipitated out by those who go to extremes when searching for truth in all aspects of a metaphor. This is another factor which casts them into darkness. It is true that there is and must be a grain of truth in every metaphor; it is this truth in which the metaphor originates and flourishes. In other words, a truth is a wick that is burned to produce light, while a metaphor is the oil lamp that feeds it. Love is in the heart, and reason is in the mind. They cannot be looked for in the hands or feet.

Another disaster which blinds the eye and veils eloquence is restriction to external meanings. Those who restrict themselves to the external meaning never turn to metaphors to search for the truth; even if they were to turn, they would look only at the expression that contains a metaphor. For this reason, interpreting some Qur'anic verses and Prophetic Traditions based on solely the external aspects of their wording cannot bring out their beauty or eloquence. Such people think that a metaphor is used where a truth would not be rationally acceptable. Yet, that which prevents a truth from being understood plainly and leads to the use of a metaphor is not only connected with the reason. Anything pertaining to human senses or other ordinary or particular means of comprehension, such as those related to addresses or arising from a speech or an article, can cause a metaphor to be used. If you would like to, enter the paradisical *Dala'il al-'Ijaz* ("Intimations of Inimitability"), chapter 221. You will see how that great genius 'Abd al-Qahir al-Jurjani[44] severely reproaches such careless people.

The sixth disaster that makes what is known unknown is when some people regard something that is accidental or which is mentioned to give extra meaning to a word as being essential. Thus, they cannot see what this addition means and remove the sun of the truth from its axis. I wonder

---

[44]   Abu Bakr 'Abd al-Qadir al-Jurjani (400–471) was a famous Muslim scholar, literary theorist and grammarian. He lived in Iran. He excelled in the two sciences of *'ilm al-balagha* (eloquence and rhetoric) and *'ilm al-bayan* (rhetoric dealing with metaphorical language). *Asrar al-Balagha* ("Secrets of Eloquence") and *Dala'il al-'Ijaz* ("Intimations of Inimitability") were his most famous works. (Trans.)

whether such people ever consider the literary style of the Arabs. For example, they say, "Mountains came across us, and then left us. They appeared before us, and then went away from us. And the sea swallowed the sun. And so on." As stated in al-Miftah by al-Sakkaki,[45] Arabs sometimes use the power of imagination, supposing that the elements of reality change places, and thus adding a subtle beauty or mystery to their words. What follows are two significant examples from the Qur'an:

> He sends down hail out of snow-laden mountains [of clouds] from the sky (24:43).

> And the sun runs the course appointed for it for a term to its resting place for the stability of it[s system] (36:38).

These two verses are worthy of attention. For freezing in the literal sense means denying eloquence its right. The metaphor in the first of the two verses is so beautiful and warm that it melts away whatever has been frozen like ice and tears up the veil of literalness. The eloquence of the other verse is so bright and fitting that it brings the sun to a stop.

The former verse contains a metaphor similar to that of *glasses, crystal-clear, made of silver* (76:15–16). The vessels of Paradise are made of neither glass nor silver. The difference between glass and silver indicates a metaphor. Glass signifies transparency, and silver, whiteness and brightness. Therefore, in order to express the transparency and brightness of the vessels of Paradise, the Qur'an uses these terms that are familiar to all people. This usage is one of the elements that encourage people to strive for Paradise. Likewise, the phrase *hail out of snow-laden mountains* contains a similar metaphor. This metaphor is based on an agreeable, delighting competition that the power of imagination conceives between the sky and the earth.

Just as the earth is shrouded with snow or embellishes itself with its mountains and multi-colored gardens, grasslands, or orchards, so too the sky, as if in competition, dresses in accumulations of clouds resembling mountains in standing separately or jointly and earthly gardens and orchards in color. If we describe these separate masses of clouds as the

---

45   Abu Ya'qub Yusuf ibn Abu Bakr al-Sakkaki (?–1229) was one of the leading scholars of the Arabic language and rhetoric. *Miftah al-'Ulum* ("Key to Sciences") and *al-Miftah fi'n-Nahw wa't-Tasrif wa'l-Bayan* ("A Key to Grammar, Inflection, and Syntax and Style") are among his most well-known works. (Trans.)

mountains or ships or camels or gardens of the sky, we are not making a bad comparison. Thunder is the captain or shepherd of those travelers (clouds) in the atmosphere. It uses lightning as its wheel or staff to drive them. The clouds which are readily driven by thunder are like mountains of carded wool on the Resurrection Day. It is as if the sky calls upon the particles of vapor to take up arms with the thunder, and scatters them with the command "At ease!" The clouds often take the shapes of mountains and appear to be like them; in the same way they also become white and cold like snow or hail, appearing as mountains shrouded in snow. What we can understand from this is that clouds and mountains are friends that have a need to be close to one another. The Qur'an, pointing to this fact, shows them sometimes in the form of the other. In addition, as they shake hands and embrace each other on the earthly page of the book of the universe, they also shake hands in several stations of the Revealed Book—the Qur'an. We frequently witness that, just as mountains are wharfs for the clouds in the ocean of the sky, the clouds anchor around the top of mountains.

As for the verse, *And the sun runs the course appointed for it for a term to its resting place for the stability of it[s system]* (36:38), the word *runs* both indicates a style and expresses a reality. The style indicated is as follows:

As if it is a glorious armored vessel constructed from gold instead of iron, the sun floats in the ocean of the sky; this ocean is formed of ether and is described as a *tightened* or *straightened* wave. Even though the sun seems to have been anchored in its orbit, this "molten gold" floats in the ocean. However, this floating is not actual; we see it floating and this indicates a reality. Nevertheless, the sun moves in two ways, but the verse under discussion does not indicate them. The reason why the verse mentions the sun as running (floating) is to emphasize the magnificent order and the fact that there is an unchanging or stable system. It does not matter whether its running has a primary or secondary place in the verse; what is being stressed here is the orderliness, the system.

Secondly, the sun moves in its ecliptic, and because of this movement, its parts of "gold"—the planets—also move. This actual movement is the mechanism of its other figurative movement under discussion.

Thirdly, wisdom requires that the sun should travel in the broad space of the world on its throne called its ecliptic, escorted by its traveling soldiers called planets. For the Divine Power has made everything movable and condemned nothing to immobility or inertia. Thus, the Divine Mercy did not bind the sun up in inertia, which is the brother of death and the cousin of non-existence. Therefore, the sun is free, and can freely travel in obedience to the Divine law, on condition that it does not violate the freedom of others.

Turning to the term *runs* in the verse discussed, it indicates the apparent but figurative movement of the sun; what gives this phrase life (that is, what helps us to understand what it truly denotes) is the phrase *li-mus-taqarrin*, which means "for the stability of it[s system]."

In short, the Divine purpose behind this expression is to show the orderliness and a stable system. The orderliness is as bright as the sun itself. Therefore, it does not matter whether this system arises from the movement of the sun or the revolution of the earth. So we have no right to question this verse as to whether the real cause of the orderliness is the movement of the sun or the earth. For example, the letter "ا (alif)" in the verb قال provides an easy pronunciation to the word. It does not matter whether the origin of this ا is و or another letter. In any case, it is ا and adds easiness to the pronunciation.

AN INDICATION

Becoming imprisoned by wording in its literal meaning is not only contrary to the warmth and beauty of eloquence, it also impedes human reason from seeing and confirming the Divine wisdom that is responsible for the excellence of the universal order, while it is human reason itself which bears witness to that wisdom. Let us give an example:

If you desire that a mountain faces you from four sides from afar, what you must do is to make four movements around yourself. But if you think or wish that this huge mountain should cover the distance and approach and then turn around you, this is certainly ridiculous and a crime committed against the order in the universe. This is what it means to be imprisoned by wording in its literal meaning without seeing or even accepting that the Qur'an uses metaphors or figures of speech. There is no waste or futility in creation, and the Qur'an reflects this, choosing the most direct way in its expressions. So, in order to adopt the most direct and understandable way, why should the Qur'an not use metaphors in a verse that expresses a reality, providing evidence of the Divine purpose for God's creation of the universe.

A REMINDER

If you like, go back to the First and Second Premises. You will see that what confuses the minds of the literalists is their attachment to Greek philosophy. They take that philosophy for their basis to understand the Qur'an. An example that could make an old woman who has lost her son laugh at their attitude is this: Despite his knowledge and care to discriminate between the genuine and the false, someone from our region said, "There are four basic elements in the universe, and angels are luminous beings created from them." He says this in order to refute the opinion of Muslim philosophers that angels are absolutely free of matter, and he is claiming that angels are bodies of (a kind of) light created from the four elements. That person and those like him think that Islam requires them to believe that existence is established upon four elements, namely air, water, fire, and earth. However, this is only an idea of ancient philosophy, not Islam. In addition, it is not necessary that everything which has some sort of relation with the Religion should necessarily be a part of it. To accept anything that is compatible with Islam as necessarily belonging to it is ignorance of the essence and essential nature of Islam. For the four basic essential sources of Islam, namely the Qur'an, the Sunna, the Consensus (of the scholars), and Analogy, neither generate such things nor form them.

In short, the acceptance of four basic universal elements of existence is a product of ancient philosophy, not of the Shari'a. Unfortunately, since the faults of that philosophy found their way into the terminology of the renowned scholars of the past, the literalists have made use of them as a reference. However, we have no evidence that those scholars who referred to the four most widespread elements believed that all existence was made up of them only. There are four other basic elements, which modern science mentions in relation to the formation of living organisms: hydrogen, oxygen, nitrogen, and carbon.

If you are a free thinker, see how ancient philosophy and science have imprisoned minds within the walls of some errors and thrown them into abjection. However, the new scientific approach has brought down the walls of that prison.

It is clear that the key to the treasure of the aspects of miraculousness in the Qur'anic verses is the eloquent language of the Qur'an. It is not to be searched for in Greek philosophy.

O brothers and sisters! Now that our curiosity to uncover secrets has taken us thus far, let us travel to the Second Part of this book, which contains the key to eloquence and miraculousness, even though I know you are tired. Do not allow the ambiguities in its style or the poverty of its garb frighten you. Their essential beauty and value and the subtlety of their meaning should be enough to justify your studying them.

The Second Part

The Essence of Eloquence

The Second Part
The Essence of Eloquence

In the Name of God, the All-Merciful, the All-Compassionate.

Eternity and all dominion is God's, and from Him are all blessings and benedictions; and blessings be upon His Prophet.

n this Part, a few matters concerning the essence of eloquence will be explained.

First Matter

(The miraculousness of the Qur'an, which is the greatest and enduring miracle of Prophet Muhammad, upon him be peace and blessings, lies primarily in its eloquence. This aspect has been the most important factor in the preservation of the Qur'an without the least change, and implies that, particularly towards the end of time, eloquence will be the most creditable means to convince people.)

As a result of many other peoples having mixed with the Arabs in the early centuries of Islam, the Mudari dialect, which was the most developed and refined dialect of Arabic and the language used in the Qur'an, became changed. In addition, eloquence came to be pursued more in the wording than in the meaning, in which the rivers of thoughts flow.

The rivers of thoughts and feelings find their natural course in the composition or arrangement of meanings. Composition of meanings is based on the principles of logic. Logic has its source in truths that are based on and corroborate one another, as well as in the thoughts that lead to these truths. The thoughts that lead to such truths penetrate the most subtle points of the natures of existent things. The most subtle points of natures are the links in the chain of the perfect order of the universe. The perfect order of the universe has a whole, abstract beauty which is the source of all the beauty of existence. This abstract beauty is the "natural" park of eloquence called literary merit and style. This park is constituted in the tunes of the nightingales—called poets—who travel in the gardens of creation and are the lovers of flowers. What gives a spiritual, effective tone to the tunes or songs of the nightingales is the composition of meanings.

Unfortunately, some non-Arabs, aspiring to be included among Arab men of letters, caused confusion. For, as the temperament of a people is the source of their feelings, in the same way, a language reflects those feelings and sentiments. Every people has a temperament particular to itself. Likewise, every language has a capacity for eloquence that is different from others. This is especially true for Arabic because it is based on strict grammatical rules. Its capacity for eloquence thus is highly different from languages that are not like it. As those who, although not Arab in origin, aspired to being counted among the Arab literary men attached greater importance to the wording than the meaning, and attachment to wording does not allow thoughts to flow along their normal course or for the flowers of eloquence to open, in this way the eloquence lost its essential purity.

The foreigners mentioned felt a greater need to write and speak beautifully and learn the literal meanings of words. Wording seems to be easier and more attractive to superficial views, and more in tune with populism; thus these foreigners concentrated their efforts on wording. Concentrating on meaning requires greater and deeper care and study. It is for this reason that the foreigners who were unable to do this became preoccupied with wording.

The meaning was left in the stage of conception, then dragged in after the wording. This caused conflicting ideas to arise. In the end, the wording received greater attention than the meaning and although wording should serve meaning, the situation became reversed with wording subjecting meaning to itself. The greater importance that was attached to wording and the more knowledge that was feigned through artificial styles, the more people became distanced from meaning. For example, you can enter the Maqamat by al-Hariri,[46] and see how his title of literary genius arose from his fascination with wording; the result was that he encouraged those who were fond of wording. In order to be able to offer a cure for this disease, the illustrious scholar of eloquence, 'Abd al-Qahir, filled one-third of his Dala'il al-'Ijaz ("Intimations of Inimitability") and Asrar al-Balaqha ("Secrets of Eloquence") with treatment. Focusing on wording is a disease, but those who suffer from it do not know that they suffer from it.

A REMINDER

Just as a fondness for wording is a disease, so also is over-concentration on form, style, simile, and rhyme a disease; and for the sake of all of these meaning is sacrificed. In our time, many literary people have written about bizarre things for the sake of a fine point or rhyme. I admit that there should be artistry in wording, but only in a manner that serves the meaning. Styles should be as attractive as possible, but remain within the frame of the meaning and the purpose of the speech or writing. Literary arts should certainly be used, but on condition that they support the truth and not damage it.

Second Matter

A word comes to life and grows when the meaning is clothed in a form and breathes speech into lifeless things through the power of imagination.

Coming into existence and becoming extinct, or birth and death, follow one upon the other. In this continuous cycle two things that exist side by side are usually perceived as the cause of the existence of the other. Any imagined or misconceived ideas that originate from that are generally the result of this perception (of the coincidence of the two things). Fantasies and the faults arising from fantasies are generally based on whims (proceeding from misunderstood perceptions). However, the magic of speech that

---

[46] Abu Muhammad Qasim ibn 'Ali al-Hariri (1024–1122) lived in Basra, Iraq. He was a scholar of Arabic language and literature. He is primarily known for the refined style and wit of his collection of tales, the Maqamat ("Assemblies"). (Trans.)

originates in the imagination breathes life into dead forms and makes them speak to one another. It can enliven the words with either love or enmity. The magic of speech also clothes meanings in forms, giving them life, and puts the heat of vitality into them.

If you want an example, read the following lines, which can be described as a house full of sound:

> Breaking one's word veils the apparent reality and tells me not to be deceived;
> So hope and despair, fighting with each other in my breast, destroy it.

See how the poet, whose words are like magic, clothes hope and despair in forms and breathes life into them, causing hostility and fighting between them because of the breaking one's word, which is a scandalous thing. One feels as if one is watching this struggle in a dream or on a screen. Truly, a magical word causes one to sleep and dream.

As another example, turn to the earth's love for rain and its lament:

> The earth complains to the rain, asking why it is late;
> It absorbs the moisture left from the last rain as if absorbing a lover's lips.

Does this couplet not make one think of the earth as a Majnun and the clouds as a Layla?[47]

A REMINDER

What makes a couplet beautiful is how close the images it contains are to reality. For when it has not rained for a long time, the earth draws in the moisture, making a sound that is almost like a sigh. One who observes this thinks of the lack of the rain and the earth's intense need for it, and considers the relationship between rain and earth. Then, one imagines the mutual love and conversation that might occur between them.

AN INDICATION

Every imagining should contain a seed of reality, like the one that exists in the couplet above.

---

[47] Majnun and Layla are legendary lovers in Oriental literature. (Trans.)

Third Matter

The fascinating garment or mold of a speech is woven on the loom of style. The beauty of speech lies in its style.

Concentration on a matter or affinity with it causes some inclinations to appear in the imagination. These inclinations take on some forms that are particular to themselves; when these come together they open a door to various comparisons, similes, and metaphors. Thus, styles that are formed of or derived from all these comparisons, similes, and metaphors are the molds of speech and the loom on which its fascinating garment is woven.

When willpower, which we can describe as the trumpet of the intellect, speaks, the meanings lying in the dark corners of the mind appear naked and head for the imagination to take on forms. Each takes on a form it finds there or, at least, wraps a scarf around its head and puts shoes on its feet. If they cannot find anything to wear at all, they pin a medal to their chest or a button, and depart, showing us in whose mind they have been trained.

If we carefully study the style of a word which has not been uttered randomly, but has emanated from the very nature of a person, it will clearly mirror the person who has dressed it. If you attempt to, based on the voice or breath that they release and the way they write or speak, understand what a person is like, and if you can imagine what kinds of things they do or how they do them, the "school" of fantasizing will not condemn you. If your imagination is afflicted with a disease that causes you to ask whether doing so is really possible, then you may end up in the hospital, which the wise doctor Busayri[48] built in the following couplet and use the prescription he wrote with repentance and tears:

> And shed tears from the eyes which have been filled
> with forbidden sights and hold on to the fasting of repentance.

Or if you have a thirst and can see how the beverage of the meaning is suited to the bottle of style, and you desire to drink it, then you can go

---

[48] Muhammad ibn Sa'id al-Busiri (Busayri) (1212–1296) was born and mainly lived in Egypt. He studied both Islamic sciences and language and literature. He is known primarily for his *Qasidat al-Burda* ("The Eulogy of the Cloak"), which he wrote in praise of our Prophet Muhammad, upon him be peace and blessings. (Trans.)

to a vintner and ask him what an eloquent word is. The art of that vintner will cause him to speak as follows:

> An eloquent word has a meaning that is fermented in the vats of knowledge, and kept in large barrels of wisdom, distilled through filters of understanding. The cupbearers, who are kind people of good taste and fine articulation, circulate the goblets of wine, and the minds partake of this offering. In this way, those meanings travel into the depths of people's inner worlds and stimulate feelings.

If you do not like the speeches of such drunkards, then you can heed the news which the Hoopoe brought to Prophet Solomon from the Queen of Sheba. Listen to how that bird, which served Solomon as a water engineer, describes the Majestic One Who sent down the Qur'an and created the heavens and the earth most beautifully, without anything preceding Him to imitate: "*I found a people who do not prostrate before God, Who brings to light what is hidden in the heavens and the earth*" (27:24–25). See how the Hoopoe mentioned God with His Attribute related to its art of engineering.

An Indication

What I mean by style is the form of the word. Others can use other words to describe the same thing. The benefit of a style is that it solders the separate statements together, forming a unity. According to the rule, "Something is established through the existence of all its parts," styles set the whole into movement by setting even only one part into movement. When a piece of writing or speech demonstrates the accomplishment of style in even a part of it, the reader or listener can sense that style throughout, albeit dimly.

For example, wherever the word "combat" is used it displays, as if through a window, a battlefield and the fighting on it. There are many words that are similar. They can be described as the cinematographers of the imagination.

A Reminder

There are many kinds and degrees of style. They are sometimes so elegant that they blow more gently than the early morning breeze. Sometimes they are more hidden than the schemes of modern diplomats. Their perception requires more than the perceptive ability of a diplomat.

For example, the commentator Zamakhshari[49] saw a challenge in the Qur'anic verse that narrates the unbelievers' rejection of the Resurrection: "*Who will give life to these bones when they have rotted away?*" (36:78) Truly, rebellious people attempt to defend themselves and even struggle against the orders of the Creator.

Fourth Matter

A word derives its power from the mutual support of its elements and from their being turned towards the basic theme. All the elements of the word should conform to the principle expressed in the adage:

> Our statements diverge, but your beauty is one;
> Each statement indicates that beauty.

A word's basic theme should be like a pool, with its elements being the streams or rivers flowing into it from all directions, so that minds will not become confused.

AN INDICATION

When all the elements of a word indicate or are turned towards its basic theme or the purpose of its utterance, order and harmony result, constituting its beauty. If you would like, consider God's Word—the Qur'an. For example, look at the following verse which dissuades people from Hellfire and shows how terrible it is:

> If but a breath from the punishment of Your Lord touches them (21:46).

See how all the elements of this verse serve the basic point by showing how intense the smallest amount of the punishment of Hellfire is and its influence upon people.

---

49 Abu'l-Qasim Jarullah Mahmud ibn 'Umar al-Zamakhshari (1075–1144) was a Mu'tazilite scholar of Islam, one among the most well-known interpreters of the Qur'an. He lived in Kwarazm. His interpretation of the Qur'an called *al-Kashshaf* was famous for its deep linguistic analysis of the verses. (Trans.)

The words "If but" (*la-in*), which start a conditional clause and contain reinforcement, signify uncertainty and therefore imply slightness (of punishment). The verb *massa* means to touch slightly, also signifying slightness. *Nafhatun* (a breath) is merely a puff of air. Being used without a definite article, it also emphasizes slightness. The double n (*tanwin*) at the end of *nafhatun* indicates indefiniteness and suggests that it is slight and insignificant. The partitive *min* (from) implies a part or a piece, thus indicating paucity. The word *'adhab* (torment or punishment) is light in meaning compared to *nakal* (exemplary chastisement) and *'iqab* (heavy penalty), and denotes a light punishment or torment. The use of *ar-Rabb* (the Lord, Provider, Sustainer), suggesting affection, instead of (for example) *al-Qahhar* (the All-Overwhelming) or *al-Jabbar* (the All-Compelling), also expresses slightness. As the entire clause expresses that this is the least amount, all of its parts reinforce that meaning.

Finally, the clause means that if such a slight breath of torment or punishment has this effect, one should reflect on how severe the Divine punishment will be. We see in this short clause how its parts are related to each other and add to the meaning. The continuing part of the verse, *they are sure to cry: "Oh, woe to us! We were indeed wrongdoers!"* also adds to the meaning or basic point of the verse.

If the slightest touch of the punishment is of such a degree, may God save us from its entirety!

A REMINDER

This is an example to you. You can weave your own lace on it. All the verses of the Qur'an have the same degree of beauty, congruence, and proportion. The purposes sometimes appear one within the other and follow each other. The connotations of each verse are side by side with those of the others, without interfering with one another. Attention is required, for a superficial view confuses many things with one another.

Fifth Matter

Just as a speech is composed in a way to express the basic idea for which it has been made, so too its beauty and depth of meaning lie in setting secondary or additional meanings and purposes to act with the help of the style that contains such literary arts as allusion, indirect reference, suggestion, and indication. With all its elements, the style stirs up the faculty of the imagination to move in various directions, and arouses feelings of appreciation in distant corners of the heart or mind. Allusions, suggestions, and indications are not intended to be the main focus; they are not made to serve the basic purpose. For this reason, a speaker is not held responsible for what allusions, suggestions, and indications are brought to mind. If you would like to, enter into the following couplets, where there are things worthy of looking on.

Look within the beard of the old man who, seated on the back of his fleet horse, desires to appear young before a young woman:

> She said, "You are old and your beard has grown white."
> I answered, "It is the dust from the events of time."

You can also look into some other couplets:

> Let not my beard glistening with grey hair frighten you;
> For it is the smile of considered views and maturity.

Another:

> Your eyes went into deep sleep in the night of youth;
> They could not wake up until the morning of old age.

Another one:

> It was as if the morning had slapped my horse in the eyes;
> My horse set off racing to reach it to avenge itself; it reached it and knocked it down with joy.

Another one:

> My heart rustles as her belt rustles while she walks;
> But her heart resembles her bracelet, which is unmoved in its place.

In the couplet above, the poet is saying that his heart beats with love for a lady but there is no love in her heart for him. He also suggests that her waist is slender and wrists are plump and round.

Another couplet:

> The flood cast its load upon the desert of Ghabt,
> As if a Yemeni merchant passed with a load of cloth.

If a Yemeni merchant comes to a village in the evening and the villagers buy his multi-colored cloth, everyone will go out next morning adorned in a different color. The herdsman of the village even wears a kerchief on his head. Likewise, when a flood casts its load upon a desert, the result of natural processes, which may be likened to an unseen biochemistry, is that multi-colored clothing is sewn for the elegant flowers. Even the cactus, which may be thought of as the shepherd of flowers, turns red.

Another:

> Faithfulness has been drawn (in a cave) and disappeared, and wronging has roared and overflowed;
> This is why there is a great distance between words and actions.

If you do not want to go further, you can take a look at the end of the first part of this book. You will find many examples of this matter. In short, the key to the miraculousness of the Qur'anic verses is Arabic eloquence; it is not ancient Greek philosophy. Or you can look at the Indication at the end of the First Matter included in the Twelfth Premise in the first part. The Divine laws of the creation and operation of the universe have stipulated that this guesthouse—the earth, which revolves in ecstasy like a Mawlawi dervish—stand in the line of the planets and obey the sun. For together with its friend—the heavens—they told God: "*We have come in willing obedience.*" (41:11)[50] Obedience and worship are better when carried out in congregation. Now, think over the examples given above. In addition to the meanings they contain, they also contain several connotations.

Sixth Matter

The fruits of a word or speech exist in its various layers of meaning, as well as in both its denotative and connotative meanings. Those who are familiar with chemistry know that when a precious metal, like gold, is obtained, the heap of earth which contains the ores is boiled down in large containers in a factory, and the matter formed is passed through many filters in the different stages of the process. In a similar way, a word has various, different meanings, which give rise to different understandings. These meanings and understandings are formed as follows:

---

[50] See footnote 37.

Some feelings and sensations appear in the heart (or mind) as a result of certain external causes. They give rise to some inclinations. Reason or intellect catches sight of certain meanings that arise from these inclinations, and draws them to itself. Some of the meanings, which are in the form of vapor, are condensed and fall drop by drop within the intellect, while others are left in the open. Some of the drops are solidified and the intellect includes them in speech. Among the solidified ones, some have particular features and the intellect gives them particular forms. As for the rest, which do not have particular features, intellect takes them parenthetically. It puts the drops that have not been solidified on the back of allusions and indications, and refers the meanings left without vaporization to the gestures of the speaker. Thus, the meanings of the speech's parts and its basic and/or general meaning, its connotations, the content, allusions, the factors causing the speech, the basic and secondary purposes for the speech, parenthetical meanings, and all other elements contained in the speech have their source in all these filters. You can see them in your own heart as follows:

When your beloved radiates the attraction and lightning of her beauty in your heart through the window of your eyes, a fire called love ignites. Feelings are aroused, and the desires and inclinations which arise make a hole in the bottom of the imagination on the upper floor and ask for help. Standing in line in the repository of imagination and immediately starting to make images when the beauty of the beloved with which they are familiar is remembered, imaginings hasten to the aid of the desires. Rushing together, they descend to the tongue from the repository of imagination. Then, putting the inclination to the sweet water of union behind them, the pangs of separation on their right, respect, description, and yearning on their left, the beauties of the beloved from which compassion and favor are begged before them and the necklace of praise and pearls of eulogies in their hands as gifts, they begin to beg the favor of union by enumerating her virtues and beauty in order to quench the fire, which can be described as the fire "which penetrates deep into the hearts."

See how many secondary meanings make themselves evident in addition to the layers of apparent meaning! If you dare to, look into the minds

of Ibn Farid[51] and Abu Tayyib[52] through their eyes, and see how the following couplets translate what is in their minds:

> I have planted a rose on her cheek with a sideways glance;
> My glance has the right to pluck the rose it has planted.

Another:

> The physician who examined my eyes and the internal organs of my
> body,
> Recited the first verse of Hal atâ, and the third verse of Tabbat.[53]

Another:

> The mole on your lip prevented me from burning for you, I do not
> know why;
> While my heart is split apart because of my attachment to you.

Another:

> My heart is in the fire kindled from a thorny tree;
> But my eyes are resting in a garden of beauties.

See the eyes looking on beauty while the heart is burning, and notice
how the couplets indicate the indifference of the beloved, the pangs of
separation, the desire and zeal for union, and praise beauty, as well as pro-
voking emotions.

AN INDICATION

Just as each official in a government department should be paid a salary
according to their capacity, the work they do, their rank, and years of

---

[51] 'Umar ibn 'Ali ibn al-Farid (1181–1235) was a Muslim Arab Sufi poet. He was born in
Cairo, lived for some time in Makka and died in Cairo. He was esteemed as one of the
greatest Sufi poets. Nazm al-Suluk ("The Poem of Journeying along the Sufi Way") and
Hamriyya ("The Ode of Wine"), which is about spiritual bliss, are his two masterpieces.
(Trans.)

[52] Abu Tayyib Ahmad ibn al-Husayn al-Mutanabbi (905–965) was born in Kufa, Iraq. He is
one of the most well-known poets in the Arabic language. He was very proud of his poetry,
scholarship, and courage. (Trans.)

[53] Hal atâ is the 76th sura of the Qur'an. The first verse reads: "Did there pass over man a stretch
of time when he was a thing not mentioned and remembered?" Tabbat is the 111th sura, and its
third verse reads: "He will enter a flaming Fire to roast." (Trans.)

service, so too the meanings in a speech that arise from different ranks should be given attention according to the relation of each to the basic purpose for the speech and the contribution it makes to that purpose. In this way the justice in this division can give rise to an order, order gives rise to proportion, proportion gives rise to mutual aid and solidarity, and mutual aid and solidarity can provide a just measure for the beauty and excellence of speech. Otherwise, those whose job is cleaning or running errands or those who have a childish temperament grow haughty because of the high rank they are given and destroy the proportion and solidarity, causing confusion. So, the capacity of each element in a speech should be considered. For despite their individual beauty, components such as the eyes or nose can make the face ugly if they are greater or smaller than the norm.

A REMINDER

A marshal may not be able to undertake the same tasks that an ordinary soldier does, for example, reconnaissance work, and a great scholar may not be able to realize the same remarkable achievement that a student can; everyone is great in their own field. Similarly, it sometimes occurs that among a multitude of meanings an insignificant seeming one becomes the most important and thus gains value. The duty of such a one is important for the following reason:

The basic element in a speech becomes either too apparent to draw any attention or too weak to serve the main purpose of the speech. Or perhaps there is no audience to lend an ear to or accept that element; or perhaps it is not compatible with the state or conditions of the speaker; or it does not serve the speaker's need or intent in making the speech; or perhaps it is not in agreement with the character or honor of the speaker; or perhaps it appears to be foreign to the main purpose of the speech or to its secondary meanings and purposes; or perhaps it is not suitable for the preservation of the purpose or the procurement of the elements that are necessary. Consequently, each of these factors may gain precedence in certain circumstances. But if all of them are present in accord with one another, they elevate the value of the speech to the highest rank.

A RESULT

There are some meanings that remain suspended, having no particular form or place. Like inspectors, they enter every department. Some take a wording particular to themselves, while others, blowing like a weak wind—another word attracts them to itself. Some words draw others to themselves. They sometimes penetrate a sentence or a brief description. When you examine that sentence or description, any of those meanings may emerge. Pains of separation, yearning, self-pride, or regret may be among those meanings.

Seventh Matter

Eloquence finds its life in, or the wisdom of speech lies in, taking the laws that operate in nature as one's guide. That is, there are laws upon which all the truths that are manifested as nature, or in nature, are dependent. These laws are unchanging, while their effects or results change either with their identities or nature. (That is, the flowers, leaves, and fruits of a tree in the present year are not the same in identity as those in the other years, but they are the same in nature.) Eloquence finds life by applying these laws to the meanings that arise in the mind, taking into consideration the changes undergone by their effects. This means that eloquence, like a mirror, dons and displays the rays of the truth that are reflected from the outer world. It is as if it wants to imitate creation and nature with the art of imagination and the embroidery of words. Even if a word or speech is not identical with the truth itself, it should receive help from the truth and the order it shapes in the outer world, and grow from the seed of truth. That is, a word or speech should use the basic truths that are manifested as nature, as the seeds to grow from. However, every seed grows into a shoot, plant, or tree peculiar to itself. A seed of wheat cannot grow to be a tree. For this reason, if the philosophy of speech is not considered, eloquence produces only superstition, and imagination only hallucination.

AN INDICATION

Like speech, grammar also has a philosophy. This philosophy, like nature, displays the Creator's wisdom. The philosophy of grammar is based on the relationship between words explained in books of grammar. For example, in Arabic, any modifiable word is modified only by the modifier that is placed right in front of it. The interrogative particle, *Hal*, wants to immediately join the verb which it modifies. The word functioning as the subject is powerful and appropriates the vowel mark *u*, which is also powerful. In short, the laws operating in languages are like the reflections of the laws operating in nature.

A REMINDER

The wisdom in the relations mentioned concerning grammar is of great value, even though it is not as clear as the wisdom of eloquence or styles. At least, it has led the traditional, reported religious sciences, such as jurisprudence, that are basically based on the explicit and implicit Revelation—the Qur'an and the Sunnah—and have developed through such principles as deduction and induction, into forms of rational science.

Eighth Matter

The meanings of a speech affect, support, and add to one another, even exchanging with and changing into one another through the essential meanings of its parts absorbing either the purpose of that speech or one of its probable meanings. The meanings left in the open change into reality, which houses the basic meaning. The meaning that gives existence to the wording or speech gains vigor and helps the other components. It also receives help from its probable connotations. For this reason, a speech has several meanings, and the exchange and relationship between the meanings arise from this point. One heedless of this fact loses a significant element of eloquence.

AN INDICATION

If, in the language of Arabic considered, something serves as a mount to get on and ride, it deserves the proposition *alā* (on) (as in the English phrases, "*on* the horse," and "*on* a train"); if it contains something else and serves as a container, it demands the proposition *fī* (in) (as in the English phrases, "*in* the room" and "*in* the dish"). If something functions as an instrument, it draws to itself the proposition *bi* (with), as in "I climbed there *with* a rope." When something serves as a place for something else or an event, it takes the preposition *fī* (in, on, or at) before it; when it has the meaning of a direction towards which something else turns or is directed to, or of a destination for which another things is headed, it requires either *ilā* or *ḥattā* (to, for). If it is something intended or a cause of an event, or if it expresses a purpose, then it is used with *li* (for), as it is in, "The sun runs the course appointed *for* it *for* a term to its resting place *for* the stability of it(s system) (36: 38)."

A REMINDER

Whichever of the concentric meanings is more connected to your purpose, give it precedence in your speech and make the other parts support it. Otherwise, your style will be devoid of splendor.

Ninth Matter

A high level of eloquence which throws simple minds and human free will into amazement and makes them unable to imitate as it has purposes one within the other and indicates the goals that are connected with one another, houses several essential elements turned towards a single result and contains many branches that bear different fruits.

The sub-purposes arising from the basic purpose support one another in order to fulfill vicinity rights, giving splendor and comprehensiveness to speech. It is as if when one appears, the others also appear. The basic purpose distinguishes all the directions (right, left, front, back, etc.) and considers the relationships among them, placing all other purposes in the fortified castle of the speech. Thus, it is as if it employs many intellects to assist it, and each purpose in the assembly of purposes is a part to which all descriptions are turned. Just as a black dot the painter adds to his painting composed of concentric pictures becomes an eye in one picture, a beauty spot in another, a mouth in still another, and so on, so too does eloquent speech have similar features.

A highly eloquent speech also considers, like an analogy starting from more than one premise that produces various results, several purposes that can be simultaneously both causes and effects in relation to each other. It is as if the speaker points to a family tree in the name of the permanence and multiplication of these purposes. For example, the world is beautiful and ordered; therefore, its Creator is Wise. He does not create in vain, nor does He waste, nor does He leave the capacities to corrupt. This means that He will constantly bring the order to perfection. He will not condemn humanity to non-existence, which means eternal separation and causes despair, prevents perfection, and is beyond endurance. So there will be eternal happiness. The differences between humanity and animals, which are discussed in the introduction to the Second Purpose in the third part of this book, are a good example of this.

A third feature of highly eloquent speech is that a single essential result it produces yields many other results and is based on different roots. Even though each root cannot be directly connected with this main, primarily intended result, at least it contributes to it. Despite the differences of the roots, the speech indicates the basic purpose embodied in the basic result and ennobles it.

A speech derives its power and vigor from its relationship with the underlying truth of universal existence, which is also called the life of the universe, universal life, or the universal conduct of affairs. "A Summation of the Most General Proofs (for Bodily Resurrection)" in the Third Purpose in the third part of this book is, to a certain extent, an example of this. In addition, the "Indication, Guidance, and Reminder" included in The Fourth Way in The Second Purpose, and the argument it contains also provide examples of this.

If you look at the Speech of the All-Merciful, Who taught the Qur'an, you will see that this truth shines in all its verses. So, woe to those who restrict themselves to their outward aspects and apparent meanings, and so ignorantly regard this aspect of the Divine Speech as repetition!

A fourth point to be mentioned concerning truly eloquent speech is that it has such a capacity and wording that there are in it seeds that can grow into many shoots, and it gives rise to many conclusions, containing many meanings and aspects. With this capacity, an eloquent speech reveals its power to produce numerous meanings and shows its products. However, it concentrates all those shoots and aspects on the basic topic for which it is intended. It also keeps its merits and beauties in balance and sends each of its shoots to a different aim, appointing each of its aspects to a different duty.

For example, the Qur'an's narrative about Prophet Moses, upon him be peace, has numerous benefits. There is much more benefit here than

the well-known kind of Arabian tree called *Tafariq Asa*, a tree which provides more and more benefit as it splits into parts. The Qur'an has taken it
in its "Bright Hand" and employs it for many purposes. It uses each aspect
of the narrative so wonderfully that those most advanced in eloquence
cannot help but prostrate before its eloquence.

O brothers and sisters! The eloquence I have tried to explain in this
section, though vaguely, portrays such a tall, majestic tree with branches
entangled with one another, the parts of which are in harmony with each
other, and which yields diverse fruits. If you would like to, you can study
the Sixth Matter. Although it is confusing, it can provide an example of
this matter.

A REMINDER AND AN EXCUSE

O brothers and sisters! I am aware that this part of the book sounds ambiguous to you. But I must keep it short and concise. It will be clarified in the
third part to certain extent.

Tenth Matter

Fluency lies in avoiding conceitedness and pursuit of superiority through
complexity and ambiguity, and therefore in not causing misconception or
confusion, and in imitating the natural order, being clear and comprehensible, not diverting from the basic point in explanations and descriptions,
and in the clarity of the purpose and the way that is followed to reach it.
Affectations or feigned sentimentality and the confusion of one's words
with other words and feelings damage fluency.

We should also avoid disordered detailing and rambling, and be careful that the arguments and meanings corroborate one another.

Again, we should be a student of nature though the power of imagination, so that the Divine laws that operate in nature may be reflected in our
work of art.

In addition, our concepts should correspond with the outer world.
Supposing our conceptions were able to leave our minds and take on forms
in the outer world, this world should be able to accept them and not deny

their origin, saying, "These belong to me, or these resemble mine, or these are my own products."

We should advance to the purpose with determination, without deviating to the right or left, so that those who stand on the side will not be able to distract us from the purpose towards themselves. Rather, those who are on the sides should contribute to the main purpose from their own beauties and riches.

Furthermore, like the pivot around which speech turns and the purpose is followed, the common meeting points of the basic and secondary purposes should be clear.

Eleventh Matter

The success and soundness of a speech lie in its ability to prove the main theme or thesis with all its elements, the foundations it is based on, and the means used to explain it. To explain something more clearly, the material used to prove the basic point or main theme should not be corrupt, and the conclusion should be put explicitly and easily. The foundations upon which the conclusion is based should be so vigorous and powerful that they should be referred to as sources and sound arguments, and they must have the necessary equipment to remove doubts and answer any possible questions.

A speech is like a fruit-bearing tree. It has thorns or "bayonets" to protect against every attack. It gives the impression that it is a conclusion drawn after long discussions and an extract obtained after many, careful acts of reasoning. Diabolical whims or doubts cannot reach it to steal from it, nor look at it maliciously. The speaker considers all the sides of this tree and has built a wall around it. He or she has also placed a guard at every point through which the speech may be exposed to attacks by creating a clear circle around the main theme and by doing his/her best not to leave any ambiguous point, or by other means of defense. Furthermore, the speaker has so equipped the speech that it has the capacity to provide answers for any possible questions.

Twelfth Matter

A speech is articulate to the extent that it is able to give the aid necessary to every fundamental part and every thought contained within it, and to clothe it in the most suitable style. If the speech is in the form of a story, the speaker or writer should play the role of the hero. If you describe the thoughts and feelings of others on behalf of the hero, then you should embody the hero or let him be a guest in your heart or speak with your tongue. But if you dispose of your own property (if you take the role of the main character), then you should consider every element of the story according to its capacity and place, cutting and sewing the dress of style according to the stature of its capacity. This will enable every secondary purpose to appear in the dress of the style most suited to it.

Style consists of three kinds for the most part:

The first is the simple, straightforward style, like the styles of Sayyid Sharif al-Jurjani and Nasir al-Din al-Tusi.[54]

The second is the ornate style, like the bright, splendid style of 'Abd al-Qahir in his *Dala'il al-I'jaz* ("Intimations of Inimitability") and *Asrar al-Balagha* ("Secrets of Eloquence").

The third is the elevated or lofty style, like some of the magnificent writings of al-Sakkaki, al-Zamakhshari, and Ibn Sina (Avicenna).

If you write about theology and methodology, you should not abandon the elevated or lofty style, which has intensity, awe, and vigor.

If you aim to persuade the audience and use an oratorical style, do not abandon the ornate style, which contains encouragement, discouragement, luster, and vivid descriptions. But you should avoid affectation.

If you write and speak on the matters included in or discussed by instrumental sciences, such as logic, mathematics, and linguistics, and the sciences of human relationships, prefer the simple, straightforward style.

In conclusion, the sufficiency of a speech lies in avoiding a style that is incompatible with the requirements of the purpose, or the occasion on which it is said, or the audience to whom it is addressed. When you want to cut and sew a style suited to the stature of the speech, you should consider why and for what purpose you are speaking or writing, the secondary

---

[54] Nasir al-Din al-Tusi (1201–1280) was one of the greatest scientists, philosophers, math - maticians, astronomers, theologians and physicians of the time and was a prolific writer. In addition, he wrote poetry in Persian. He was born in Tus near the present Mashhad. The observatory at Maragheh, which he built, became operational in 1262. He wrote one or several treatises on different sciences such as geometry, algebra, arithmetics, trigonometry, medicine, metaphysics, logic, ethics, and theology. (Trans.)

purposes you are aiming at, the audience you are addressing, and the circumstances in which you are speaking; you should not break off from the main way by lending your view and attention to side issues, and not waste your "wealth." Just as a speech displays the meaning through its purpose, arts, and the occasion on which it is said, style also indicates the meaning, and the meaning, arts, and the occasion on which the speech is said, all contribute to the style.

If you would like to, you can look into the introductions to the works written about the topics included in or discussed by elevated sciences such as theology and Qur'anic interpretation. Even though every introduction does not have the same degree of eloquence, each of them vividly and clearly expresses the main purpose of the work.

A Conclusion

They say we should consider what is spoken, not the speaker. But I say that eloquence requires considering all of these points: Who says it? To whom is it said? On what occasion is it said? On what authority is it said? For what purpose is it said?

An Indication

Eloquence requires that the main purpose for a speech or piece of writing should sometimes specifically and sometimes allusively be referred to, and whatever is said or written should flow towards it. Occasional and coincidental references to the main purpose are of no use.

Literary devices, such as similes, metaphors, and allegories, should not be used for their own sake, but should be used when the style requires them.

An Explanation

When used for certainty, the particle *inna* (surely, assuredly) is the most precise and decisive of the words indicating a concrete reality in the outer world and connecting a conceptual proposition with the relevant law in nature. It is for this reason that the Qur'an frequently uses it.

A REMINDER AND AN EXCUSE

O brothers and sisters! Let my puzzling style not distract you from the truths expounded in this book. One who is a specialist in a branch of science is not expected to be a specialist in all the branches. Also, centripetal force is greater than centrifugal force, and the ears are nearer to the mind than the tongue and are related to reason. In addition, the heart, which is the origin of words, is distant from the tongue and is a foreigner to it. Furthermore, the tongue is usually unable to understand the language of the heart. If the heart in particular speaks as if from the bottom of a well, the tongue cannot hear it and therefore cannot interpret it.

In short, understanding is easier than describing. However, I beg your forgiveness for my ambiguous style, and noble hearts are forgiving.

You can take the First Part of this book as a primary and the Second Part as a secondary premise and, allowing intuition to conduct through them like an electric current, begin to read the Last Part, which is about some matters of belief.

The Third Part

The Element of Belief

The Third Part
The Element of Belief

In the Name of God, the All-Merciful, the All-Compassionate.

I bear witness that there is no deity but God, and I also bear witness
that Muhammad, upon him be blessings and peace, is His Messenger.

hile this elevated proclamation is the basis of Islam, it is also
the loftiest and most luminous flag waving in the heavens.
The belief, which is a pledge we gave to God in pre-eternity
and through which we are bound to God, is epitomized in
this sacred proclamation. And Islam, which is the pure water of life, has its
source in this pure spring. This proclamation is an eternal "royal decree"
given into the hands of those who among humankind have been appointed to the palace of eternal happiness which they have been promised. It is
also the luminous map of the heart, which is the spiritual faculty given to
humans by the Lord, the King of Eternity, to know and make Him known,
and to believe in Him, and as a window that opens on the worlds of the
Unseen. Furthermore, it is a fluent orator, presenting the mysterious, eloquent oration of the conscience to the whole universe, and an eternal
decree at the disposal of the tongue, which is an eloquent herald of belief,
announcing the Eternal Sovereign to the universe.

AN INDICATION

Each of the two parts of this elevated proclamation is a true witness and proof
for the other. God's existence and Oneness, or Divinity, is *a priori* proof for

the Messengership; Divinity demands one who will make God known to others; and Prophet Muhammad, who represents the Messengership in all its dimensions and entire comprehensiveness, upon him be peace and blessings, is *a posteriori* proof for Divinity with his person, life, and mission.

A REMINDER

The truths of Islamic belief have been detailed in all their aspects in relevant Islamic books. So they are clear enough for all to perceive. Since attempting to show what is already clear and obvious may be regarded as taking the audience for a fool, I will explain only a few elements of Islamic belief. I refer the reader to the works of scholars for the rest.

Introduction

It is well known that the Qur'an has four basic purposes, or pursues the establishment of four cardinal truths: The existence of the Oneness of the Creator, the Prophethood, bodily Resurrection, and Worship and Justice.

One of the proofs that establishes the Creator's existence is Prophet Muhammad, upon him be peace and blessings. In fact, God's existence and Oneness is so clear that it is far above needing discussion or proof. But since many people are thrown into doubt about this most manifest truth, and since some Japanese people (visiting Istanbul) asked me about it, I feel obliged to write about this truth. They ask: What is the clearest proof for the existence of the Deity to Whom you call us. What has existence been created from—from non-existence, or matter, or the Essence of that Deity?

AN INDICATION

As the proofs for God and signs for knowledge of Him are innumerable, it is impossible to describe Him in only a few words. So I beg forgiveness for my inability to explain the matter as clearly as required.

A REMINDER

What I intend is to be able to show the way to sound, balanced reasoning, so that the resulting truth will appear clearly at the end of the article. Otherwise, skepticism, which is supported by the desire to see the result in every part of the article, and which is opposed by the inability of the human mind to show the intended result in every part of speech or writing, will cause the truth to be hidden in doubts and whims.

Under the influence of some negative factors such as biased and willful opposition or self-centeredness, humans have a tendency to excuse themselves by basing their groundless suspicions and whims on a reality. In addition, they look for pretexts. Also, a customer usually finds defects or faults with something they will buy. All these factors prevent one from seeing or admitting the truth. If you are not prevented by such obstacles, you may try nevertheless to listen to me with a peaceful heart.

The First Purpose

While every atom that has ever had and will ever have a place in the construction or composition of the universe is suspended among infinite possibilities as to where and when and how it will go and settle, the atom suddenly follows a definite direction, and finds its exact place, producing amazing results. This bears witness to the existence of One with absolute, all-encompassing Knowledge, Will, and Power. Through this testimony, the lamp of belief in the Creator within the heart is also kindled, as this faculty is an epitome of the worlds of the Unseen. As each atom announces the Creator by itself, it also shows His Wisdom through its relationships with all the other atoms which form the compounds or compositions of particular things, as well as with many other elements of existence. These relationships give many purposeful and beneficial results, and serve the magnificent, indestructible balance of existence. This brings us to the conclusion that the proofs for the existence of the Creator are much more numerous than the atoms that make up the universe.

If you ask why everyone does not see God with the eyes of their reason or intellect, I will answer that He cannot be seen because of the intensity of His manifestation. There are many material things that, because of the intensity of their manifestation, are beyond the scope of human sight or which can make humans blind. The All-Majestic Creator is absolutely free of being material, so how can He be seen?

> Ponder over the lines of the universe,
> For they are letters to you from the highest realm.

Look at the chains of events and things with which the Eternal Embroiderer decorates all of the vast universe; look with the eye of wisdom, so that the letters coming to you in uninterrupted series from the highest realm may cause you to rise to the zenith of a degree of certainty of belief.

AN INDICATION

Human conscience does not forget the Maker due to the point of reliance and the innate request for help. Even though the mind sometimes ceases to work, taking a temporary vacation, the conscience never does. It is always occupied with two jobs, which are as follows:

When resorted to, the conscience shows that, just as the heart dispenses life throughout the body, so too knowledge of God (ma'rifetullah), which is the source of life in the heart, deals out life to infinite tendencies and ambitions that humans have in proportion to their capacity. The conscience expands these, giving them value and putting pleasure in them. This is the innate request for help of the human conscience.

In addition to this, the sole point of reliance for humans against the tumults, difficulties, sufferings, and calamities that attack life, one after the other, is knowledge of the Creator.

If humans do not believe in the All-Wise Maker Who does everything wisely and in orderly fashion, and instead blindly attribute everything to supposed coincidences, they will find themselves in a hellish state of loneliness, dread, worry, and fear, in which they will be aware of how little power they have in the face of calamities. Even though they are the most honored of creatures, they will be more miserable than other beings. This also contradicts the essence of the magnificent order of the universe. So the sole refuge or point of reliance for the human is knowledge and recognition of God.

As these two points, namely the point of reliance and the inner request for help, are among the basic elements and essential realities in the order of the universe, the existence of the Maker shows itself through their windows in the human conscience. Even if human reason does not see Him, the conscience sees Him through the heart, which is its window.

The Ways Leading to Knowledge of God

There are four ladders or ways to reach knowledge of the Creator, which is the highest point human beings can reach:

The first is the way of the scholarly Sufis, which is based on purification of the soul, refinement of the heart, and intuition or inner observation.

The second is the way of the theologians. It is based on two arguments. The first is that the existence of the universe is possible, but not necessary. This is because it is contained in time and space, or is accidental or contingent. So there must be One Who willed its existence and brought it into existence. The second argument is that the universe is not timeless or without beginning; it has a beginning, and this requires the existence of a timeless One Who brought it into existence.

Both of these ways are derived from the Qur'an, but human thought has given them their own forms and therefore elaborated on them.

The third way belongs to the people of wisdom or the believing philosophers. This way is open to controversy and the attack of whims or suspicion.

The fourth is the way of the Qur'an, which is the most direct and the clearest of ways, one which shows the peerless eloquence of the Qur'an and is possible for everyone to follow. The following argument explains the two most important steps on this ladder:

THE FIRST QUR'ANIC ARGUMENT

The first is the argument of assistance, beneficence, and purposefulness. All the Qur'anic verses that mention the benefits of things and the purposes they serve indicate or are comprised of this argument. This argument is based on the fact that the perfect universal order takes into account beneficence and purposefulness. Whatever exists serves many benefits and purposes and has many instances of wisdom. This categorically rejects and negates the assertions of chance or coincidence.

Everyone may not be able to reach the Creator through the way of the order of the universe or the purposes of its existence; it is also possible that they may not be able to perceive this order or these purposes. But it is a fact that human thought and the investigations that support one another over the course of history have led to the foundation of sciences, each of which examines one part of the Book of the Universe or a species of existence, and comprises the general rules and principles concerning that species. Where there is no order, it is impossible to deduce or discover general rules and principles. So, since there are such rules and principles that are in effect in the existence and lives of every species, this clearly shows that there is a specific order in every corner of the universe. The sciences based on general rules and principles are proof for the perfect order of the universe.

By showing the benefits and purposes attached to the chains of things and beings and the instances of wisdom in the series of changes and revolutions that occur over the course of the days, months, seasons, years, centuries, and ages, the sciences indicate and testify to the universal purpose and wisdom of the Maker, functioning as meteors that destroy the devils of doubts and whims.

AN INDICATION

Familiarity causes compounded ignorance and superficial views. Purposeful opposition and the attitude maintained to silence others for the sake of obstinacy, caused by a refusal to accept the truth, is a nest of whim and suspicion that blocks the way of reason. If you are saved from such familiarity and purify your soul of sheer opposition in the name of obstinacy due to a refusal to accept the truth, you will not be able to persuade your soul that the miraculous mechanism working in the form of a microscopic animal is the product of what you call natural causes and laws. Clearly, these causes or laws are blind, lifeless, and unconscious, and they have no knowledge about what they must do and where, when, why, and how they will do it. Nor do they have free will. Were you to attribute to them creativity, then you would have to accept that every atom has much greater consciousness and wisdom than Plato and much more knowledge than Galileo, and believe that every atom communicates directly with all other atoms, and that the forces of attraction and repulsion in atoms form, on their own, a channel through which they meet. If your soul can consider the possibility of such inconceivable things, can you really be considered to be a human being endowed with a well-functioning mind? Rather, you should think that what you call natural causes and laws are the results or descriptions of God's acts or the veils He has made before His actions; the laws, which have a nominal existence, should not be seen as active natural forces that have a creative effect in the universe.

A REMINDER

Look yet again: can you see any rifts? (67: 3)

Look around the universe; where can you see a fault or a rift? One who has sound eyes will not be able to see any. If you like to, turn to the Qur'an. You can find in it the argument of assistance, beneficence, and purposefulness in the most perfect fashion. For the Qur'an both orders that we reflect on the universe and mentions the benefits of things and God's innumerable blessings. All the relevant verses are mirrors of the argument of assistance, beneficence, and purposefulness.

THE SECOND QUR'ANIC ARGUMENT

The second basic Qur'anic argument for God Almighty's existence and Oneness is that of creation or origination. Its summary is as follows:

Every species and all members of every species have been given an existence according to the function or purpose assigned to each and the capacity accorded to each. In addition, no species is a link in a chain that stretches back to the eternity of the past, for their existence is contingent or accidental, not absolute. There is a Will that makes a choice between their existence and nonexistence, and a Power that gives them existence. Existence is clearly not timeless but is contained in time and space, and therefore has a beginning.

A FALSE SUPPOSITION AND A REMINDER

A truth cannot become its opposite, nor can its nature change. There cannot be any intermediary species between existing species. The transformation of a species into another means the complete transformation of an established truth, which is impossible.

AN INDICATION

Every species came into existence separately and has an original ancestor. Sciences such as zoology, geology, and botany testify to this fact. Besides, neither the material causes, nor nature, nor any other "law," supposed, nominal, or real, can have any creative part in the things that come into existence. Every species and every member of a species is created by the All-

Wise Maker, individually and separately. The All-Majestic Maker has put on the forehead of everything the stamps of "contingency" and "having a beginning" or "being contained in time and space."

A REMINDER

Claiming that matter is eternal and the motion of particles or atoms is the origin of all species that exist is contingent upon an unawareness of or indifference to the Creator, or results from being caught up in a false state of unawareness while searching for the truth, or is the intentional appropriation of a contradictory stance due to certain motives. If a person who had accepted this fallacy can reevaluate it after having found the truth, they can understand what a false, impossible proposition they had accepted.

A REMINDER

Humanity is noble by creation; it is for this reason that we always want to take hold of the truth and pursue happiness. Humans find falsity or misguidance in their hands unawares while searching for the truth; or at a time when they are tired of searching for the truth, their soul will be forced to accept something unreasonable or impossible because of a misguided or deflected view or glance. Pay attention to this point. You will see that human conscious nature categorically rejects those who attribute eternity to matter and movement when explaining the origin of existence by ignoring the perfect order of the universe; and those who maintain that all is coincidence or chance, despite the amazing, miraculous art and embroidery in every single thing and in the entirety of creation; and those who ascribe creativity to material causes and what they call laws, in spite of sound thought and reasoning and an unbiased scientific approach; and those who think that they have found consolation in attributing existence to nature because of the regularity in things and events, despite the opposite judgment of their conscience. The reason why they act in opposition to their conscious nature is that while they are advancing on the path to the truth, false whims and suppositions attack them from both sides. Since they advance with the aim of reaching out the truth awaiting them at the end of the path, they only take a side glance at those whims and suppositions. Therefore, they cannot see their corrupt or putrid nature. If they were aware, they would not purchase such ideas, nor would they even lower themselves to glance at them.

The conscience or human conscious nature rejects such assertions and sound reason sees them as being impossible. But demagogy and addiction to opposition and controversy may lead one to accept them, while this means that one asserts that in each atom exists the intellect of the wisest philosophers and scientists and the administrative ability and sagacity of the most eminent rulers, and that all atoms are in continuous consultation and communication with one another. This is the basic characteristic of falsehood. When people take a sideways look at or have an imperfect view of something or when that thing captures the corner of their eye, they may then assert that falsehood is true. But if they concentrate on it, examining it directly and soundly, they will see its true nature.

An Indication

Matter cannot be thought of as being separate from the changing form and the movement which appears and disappears over time. So it is not eternal; it is contained in time. How ridiculous then that there are those who cannot accept the existence and eternity of the Maker, Whose existence is absolutely necessary for the universe to come into existence and for it to continue to exist, yet, at the same time, they can attribute eternity and creativity to matter, which is lifeless, unconscious, and absolutely devoid of knowledge and will-power. How strange it is that some, who although members of humanity, cannot ascribe the universe, which is wonderful in all its parts and in its totality, to the Maker, Who has all the attributes of perfection, but rather ascribe it to lifeless, unconscious, and blind chance and the motion of atoms, which are also lifeless, blind, and unconscious.

An Explanation

With respect to their essence, the species are different from one another. Neither the forms nor the forces, which are claimed to be produced through the motion of atoms, nor the nuclei of cells, can be responsible for this essential difference. For all of these are accidental to the essence; they themselves are the results of the differences of the essence. This shows that all the species with their differences were brought into existence separately by a Creator, Who does whatever He wills however He wills. If you desire further explanations concerning the argument of creation or origination, you can enter the paradise of the Qur'an, where you can find every truth, either in the form of blossoming flowers or as buds or as seeds.

A FALSE SUPPOSITION AND A REMINDER

If you ask what "nature" is, a question that is frequently asked, and if you ask what are those things that they call "forces of nature" to which they attribute everything, my reply is as follows:

God has a collection or an assembly of His laws called "the laws of creation and the operation of the universe," which are in fact God's acts of creating and regulating and putting in order the corporeal world with whatever is in it and the functions of its "members" and "organs." This assembly of the laws of the creation and the operation of the universe is like an immaterial Divine printing machine, but they call it nature. What they call "the laws of nature" are those acts of God or the sum of their effects; and what they call "the forces" are the ways they are carried out. The regularity of their execution or the formation of a collective, imaginary body in the mind that is caused by their execution, or by the incessant, rapid movement of their execution that cannot be observed, causes people to attribute external existence to this assembly of laws and the effects of their implementation. What they call nature is this imagined external existence.

AN INDICATION

Those things they call nature and natural forces are not able to be the origin of existence, nor can they be accepted as such by a sound mind or by the truth. But the obstinacy of not accepting the existence of the Creator and the regularity of His acts which are responsible for the creation and operation of the universe may lead some to attribute these amazing works of the Divine Power to what they call nature. However, nature is, in fact, a print; it is not the printer; it is a tune, not the composer; it is a design, not the designer; it is a recipient, not the agent; it is an order, not that which gives the order. It is a collection of laws established by the Divine Will, not a power.

AN ILLUMINATION

If a being were to come to this world from another planet and be totally ignorant of this world, they might see the socio-political order or the laws which order human social actions as a spiritual guide or an invisible ruler who prevents conflicts and sedition in the society. Similarly, if such a one were to see the ordered, repeated actions or movements of a soldier or a troop of soldiers, they might think that there were invisible ropes between the members of the troop that connected them to one another; could we honestly say that this is strange? Likewise, do people criticize a Bedouin or a natural poet who gives a bodily existence in his mind to the system that connects people and regulates their actions, which he regards as a spiritual sovereign? So, therefore, if the collection of Divine laws or the regulations of the Divine acts responsible for the miraculously ordered operation of the universe—and there are no exceptions to these apart from God's special dispensations to be used as miracles to prove the Prophethood of His Prophets in the sight of people or as wonders to honor His saints—if that collection of laws or the regulations of Divine acts are clothed in a body in some imaginations, we should not deem it strange. What is really strange is that some attribute to it the acts of the All-Knowing, All-Willing, and All-Powerful Creator and Lord of the worlds.

A FALSE SUPPOSITION AND A REMINDER

Humanity is usually unable to see or study something in its totality or as a complete entity. It tends to compartmentalize everything or divide it into parts, and then examine it. Humanity first concentrates on a single part, and then passes onto the other parts. In addition, the value of humans is proportional to the nature and greatness of their ideals and the exertion of their efforts to realize them. They are usually lost in their aspirations and the things with which they are occupied. It is for this reason that insignificant things and deeds are not attributed to a great being. It is generally accepted that greatness does not allow one to be occupied with insignificant things. Further, humans search for the standards of evaluating the thing with which they are occupied first in themselves and, if they cannot find it in themselves, then they search for the same in others like themselves. Even if they think about the Necessarily Existent Being, Who does not resemble any of the created in any way, they attempt to judge Him according to the particular standards they find in themselves or in others. However, the All-Majestic Maker can never be "observed" or judged from the viewpoint of human beings. His Power has no limits at all. His Power, Knowledge, and Will encompass and penetrate everything. Consider that even the sun, which is a material body among numberless heavenly objects that have been created by God, Who has nothing in common with matter or being material, penetrates everything within the vast expanse of the reach of its light. We do not have anything with which we can weigh or compare the All-Majestic Maker's Knowledge, Will, and Power. They simultaneously penetrate and encompass every single thing, no matter how vast or how minute. As they penetrate and encompass the universe as a whole, they also penetrate and encompass all individual parts of it at the same time. So, to compare the Necessarily Existent Being to any of the created entities is completely erroneous. Nevertheless, falling into this error, naturalists ascribe creativity to material causes or what they call nature and natural forces; the Mu'tazilites held that living beings were the creators of their own actions; the Muslim Peripatetic philosophers asserted that Divine Knowledge does not encompass individual small entities or particles of existence; the Zoroastrians believed in two separate deities, one as the creator of good, and the other as the creator of evil. They deemed it unbecoming to the limitless Grandeur and Dignity of the All-Majestic Maker that He should occupy Himself with what they regard as small and insignificant. This false notion captivated them. O brothers and sisters! Some believers can be vulnerable to such false notions in the form of unintentional suggestions.

AN INDICATION

You can say: "The evidence of creation from non-existence is creation itself or giving existence to something non-existent, and giving existence to something non-existent is a brother or sister of making something existent non-existent. But we cannot comprehend the possibility of creation from non-existence or the making of something existent non-existent." I will reply as follows:

Your incomprehension issues from a misleading comparison. For you conceive of God's creation of existence from non-existence, with nothing preceding Him, as an imitation of the acts of the created. No creature is ever able to give existence to something that does not exist or to make something that is existent non-existent. What conscious, living beings can do is imitation or bringing the parts together to form a new composition or a complete entity, or dividing a whole into parts.

Since humans have never seen the like of the Divine Power in the universe, they cannot comprehend God's creation of existence from non-existence or His causing something that exists to cease to exist. The rational arguments of human beings and the conclusion they draw are based on observations. They view the Creator's acts and works from the perspective of the acts and works of the created, and make a misleading comparison between them. However, they should view the Creator's acts and works with the consideration in mind of His limitless Power.

AN INDICATION

While thinking about the works of a person, we should take their attributes into consideration; we should view their works from the perspective of that person's personal attributes. If we view God's acts and works from the perspective of the attributes (power, capacity, and knowledge) of the created, we can only arrive at a wrong conclusion. One of the reasons for conceiving the impossibility of creation from non-existence and the making of something existent non-existent is this incorrect viewpoint. Everyday we witness innumerable instances of creation from non-existence. (That material causes have a part in creation from non-existence should not deceive us, for they have no part in the giving of life, which is purely a gift of the Creator. In addition, every day many things occur, the causes of which science cannot explain.) Despite these facts, those who see creation from non-existence as being impossible compare the Divine Being and His Attributes and acts with the created, and want to see that which is essentially invisible.

A REMINDER

If we approach the matter not from the perspective of creation from non-existence but from the viewpoint of reproduction or creating existence from matter, the most obvious example of the things created or brought into existence from a substance is light. The amazing laws that operate in the existence of light and the light of eyes or the mechanism of sight show the perfection of Divine Power. Thus, if we approach the act of creation from the perspective of the perfection of Divine Power, we will easily be able to accept many things which we are unable to comprehend even superficially.

A REMINDER

Just as in logic theories are produced from premises, which are universally true rules or principles, so too do the "premises" in the works of the Maker suffice to see and explain the hidden points in His Art. This proves creation from non-existence.

AN EXPLANATION

Can reason conceive of something more beautiful, more subtle, more unequaled, or more impossible for the created than the art displayed by the perfect system and orderliness of the universe? Certainly not. Sciences show the benefits of this system with all its parts and the purposes of their existence, thus proving that nothing is in vain or purposeless in creation. This manifest fact testifies to the art and wisdom of the Maker in creation, and leaves reason with no alternative but to accept His existence. When reason is left to its own devices without the enlightenment of such obvious realities, particularly under the influence of the evil-commanding soul, it denies even such clear realities.

Why can the All-Holy Being, Who has created the heavens and the earth and holds them suspended, Who has put everything in order and made them subservient to His commands, not make things easier? It is sheer fallacy to claim that a power that can lift up a mountain cannot move or lift up an inkpot. In short, just as the verses of the Qur'an interpret one another, the book of the universe, or its "verses," also interpret the art and wisdom that rests under its lines.

AN INDICATION

You say: The words of some Sufis imply agglutination and contiguity with the Divine Being, or Union, or Incarnation. These seem to be identical with ideas like pantheism or monism.

Answer: Such words attributed to the verifying, scholarly Sufis are uttered in a state of spiritual ecstasy and allegorical. Therefore, they require interpretation. Since these people are immersed in the manifestations of the Divine Being's Existence, they see the result in the evidence on which they concentrate. That is to say, looking through the windows of the universe, they find themselves completely surrounded by the manifestations of the Maker in the channels of coming into and going from existence; concentrated in the realms beyond the veils of things, they see only the flow of Divine gifts in things; and looking into the mirrors of existence, they only observe the manifestations of the Divine Attributes and Names. Due to a lack of appropriate words to express their observations, they use terms such as Pervasive Divinity and Pervasive Life. Those lacking in sufficient knowledge of the matter, those who approach their words only from the perspective of the terms they use, apply their own whims and supposition to these words. The transcending observations and standpoints of the verifying, scholarly Sufis are infinitely superior to the suppositions of materialist imitators. Viewing these two infinitely different approaches and standpoints to be identical or near to each other means the declaration of the death of reason in this age of progress. True humanity feels obliged to say with the tongue of verification and progress in the face of such attitudes, "No, by God, no! How can the Pleiades shining in the sky be found through the bottom of the earth? How can the bright, piercing light be compared with veils of darkness?"

AN INDICATION

The doctrine of the verifying, scholarly Sufis, which is figuratively called the Unity of Being, is, in fact, the Unity of the Witnessed (the existence and absolute Unity of the Divine Being manifested in and testified to by the creation as a whole, united entity and with all its parts interconnected with one another). The Unity of Being in its literal meaning and content is the false doctrine of some ancient philosophers.

A REMINDER

The chief of the Sufis mentioned says, "One who claims contiguity with the Divine Being or Union (with Him) or Incarnation (of Him) has not the least share in knowledge of God." How can something that is contingent, which is absolutely in need of one who prefers its existence to its non-existence, be in union with the Necessarily Existent Being? The truth is that a contingent being bears some of the manifestations of the Divine Being. But this is in no way proof of a relation between the Sufis' doctrine of the Unity of the Witnessed with the materialists' doctrine of the Unity of Being, the latter of which amounts to pantheism or monism. For according to the doctrine of the materialists, matter is essential and the origin of existence. For this reason, materialists who maintain this doctrine are impeded from understanding the truth of Divinity. Since they are lost in matter, they deviate and attribute everything to matter, seeing matter as being the Divine Attribute of Creation. But the exacting, scholarly Sufis concentrate totally on the Existence of the Necessarily Existent One and totally ignore the contingencies. So these two doctrines are completely opposed to each other. Nothing can be worse or more condemnable than perceiving them as being identical with or approximate to each other.

AN ILLUMINATION

Supposing that the earth consists of small, multifarious, multicolored pieces of glass, each of these pieces receives a manifestation of the sun according to its shape, color, and size. But the reflected sun in one of these pieces is not identical to the sun nor is the reflected light same as the light of the sun. Similarly, if the colors of multi-colored flowers, which (according to a theory) reflect the colors in the spectrum of the light of the sun, were able to speak, each would say, "The sun resembles me," or "I am the sun itself."

> Such images are snares for saints;
> They are the reflections of the bright-faced ones in God's garden.

The way of the people of the Unity of the Witnessed is the way of the saints who live immersed in and intoxicated by the manifestations of the Necessarily Existent Being. The safest way is that of the scholarly saints who can, even though they go into ecstasies with the manifestations of the Divine, maintain the balance between the manifestations of God's Essential Qualities, Attributes, and Names, and clearly see the infinite dissimilarity between the Creator and the created.

How can a human being, someone who cannot perceive their own nature, perceive what the Eternal, All-Compelling is like? It is He Who brings things into existence with there being nothing preceding to imitate, and gives each thing an exact proportionate form; how can one who has been brought into existence within time perceive Him?

A REMINDER

The preceding notes are a summary of the proofs for the existence of the Maker. If you would like to hear about the proofs of His Oneness, they are infinite. Here, I can mention only one of them, which is expressed in a verse of the Qur'an, *Had there been in the heavens and the earth any deities other than God, both (of those realms) would certainly have fallen into ruin* (21: 22). The proof derived from this verse is called the Proof of Prevention. Absolute independence is indispensable to Divinity.

AN ILLUMINATION

The facts that there are many essential similarities among existent things and beings; and that all these beings and things and the elements comprising the universe exist together without any confusion; and that all these beings, things, and elements display perfect orderliness, come to the aid of one another in perfect solidarity, and move around the focal point upon which the order of the universe is based—these are all clear proofs for the Oneness of the Maker, the Eternal and All-Wise One.

There is a sign in every and each thing that proves the fact that He is One.

> The pages of the Book of the Universe—they are dimensions limitless;
> The lines written through the events happening within time—they are works countless.
> Printed on the press of the Supreme Preserved Tablet,
> Everything in the universe is a meaningful, embodied word.

In the stanza above, Hoja Tahsin is speaking of a relative infinity and multiplicity; he is not referring to an actual infinitude.

AN INDICATION

However many attributes of perfection there are, the Maker of Majesty has them. Any perfection the creation displays is a dim shadow of His Perfection.

He has Attributes of Perfection, Beauty, and Grace beyond all concepts and modalities. All instances of favoring observed in the universe point to His infinite Wealth and Generosity just as all instances of existence indicate His Existence; answering the calls and performing one's prayers is the response to the absolute necessity of His Existence, and all beauty indicates His Beauty. In addition, the Maker of Majesty is infinitely exempt or free from any defects or shortcomings. He is infinitely free from any defects that originate in the insufficiency of the inherent capacities of creation and from the needs that arise from the contingent nature of the universe.

There is nothing that resembles Him; Exalted is His Majesty.

The Second Purpose

INTRODUCTION

You ask: You say that the second part of the Proclamation of Testimony—I bear witness that there is no deity but God; and I also bear witness that Muhammad is His servant and Messenger—is a witness for the truth of the first part, and the first part is a witness for the truth of the second part. Is this really so?

Answer: Yes, this is so. The safest and the truest of the ways that lead to knowledge of God, which is the "Ka'ba" of perfections, is the soundest and most radiant one which was built by the holy resident of Madina al-Munawwara, upon him be peace and blessings. That resident, Prophet Muhammad, upon him be peace and blessings, is the spirit of right guidance, his heart is the lamp that illuminates the unseen worlds. His truthful tongue, which is the translator of his heart, is the most articulate and truest of the proofs of the Maker's existence and Oneness. His being and his words are both a light-diffusing proof. Prophet Muhammad, upon him be peace and blessings, is the most decisive and undeniable proof of the Maker, of the institution or mission of Prophethood, of the Resurrection and the afterlife, and of the truth.

A REMINDER

It is not necessary to refer to the proofs of the existence and Unity of the Maker in order to prove the truth of that holy being, Prophet Muhammad, upon him be peace and blessings.

An Establishment

Our Prophet is a proof for the Maker. So we should analyze this proof from certain, essential viewpoints.

In the Name of God, the All-Merciful, the All-Compassionate.

O God! Bestow blessings and peace upon Muhammad, who bears witness to the absolute necessity of Your existence.

O lover of truth! If you would like to look through the window of conscience or human conscious nature, first do not assume the attitude of intentional opposition, which causes the faculty of the heart to be polluted and rust. Also, do not lend an ear to your whims and fancies, nor expect something that should be given by a community to come from every member of that community. Expecting something from every member of a community causes the denial or rejection of the result. This is a point that requires close attention.

In addition, you should purify the mirror of your heart from childish attitudes and enmity, both of which tend to searching for and taking shelter in pretexts. Also, do not look through the eyes of the customer who sees only defects and failings. Furthermore, when you weigh, weigh accurately; compare correctly. What is more, take for evidence and guidance the shining light of truth that comprises all the signposts along your way, so that you can dispel the darkness of groundless doubts and whims that may appear. Finally, listen with an attentive, careful ear, and do not object before my words are finished. All that I will utter amounts only to a sentence. When I have said all of it, you can voice your objections, if you have any.

A Reminder

One dimension of this proof is Prophethood in general; the other is the Prophethood of Muhammad, upon him be peace and blessings.

An Indication

The Maker does nothing without a purpose; there are many instances of wisdom in His every act. There is an order in everything in the universe, down to the things that are seemingly the most insignificant. Nothing is neglected in creation, and humanity needs a guide on its way to eternity. All these realities demonstrate the necessity of the institution of Prophethood.

If you would like this argument to be explained, then listen:

You can see that there is an order in creation, including the world of humanity, as well as in the animal kingdom, many members of species of which have been put in the service of humanity because of the reason given to humanity. Humanity's superiority to animals in the following three points is a proof of the necessity for Prophethood:

The first is the interesting reality of the fact that the beginning of thought is the end of action, and the beginning of action is the end of thought. That is, actions give rise to thoughts, which, in turn, lead to actions. Humanity has the capacity to be able to see the relationship between the cycles of causes and effects. In the light of this relationship, it arrives at new combinations and the forms or rules of new thoughts and behavior, as well as what we call laws which appear to be responsible for cause and effect. This is the mechanism of progress and evolution. Science is the ability to analyze those combinations, or to be able to detect the individual elements and causes and effects, which form or lead to them, and the laws that appear to be responsible. Based on these laws, humanity can develop or produce new things. However, its capacity is limited, and its abilities are defective. Thus, together with these defective and limited capacities and abilities, the desire to satisfy all of humanity's needs, and humanity's innate ignorance and powerlessness, as well as the fancies, caprices, suspicions, and whims that pester it constantly, cause us to be in absolute need of the guidance of Prophethood. Only through Prophethood can the perfect orderliness of the universe, with whatever is in it and whatever occurs in it, be perceived adequately. The balance and order of human life depend on the ability to perceive this universal order.

The second point is that humanity has been equipped with a great potential and has almost limitless ambitions and tendencies, barely controllable thoughts and conceptions, and the faculties of lust and anger which have not been restricted in origin, but which require education or training and restraint. This essential dimension of human existence also requires Prophethood.

AN INDICATION

Even if a person were given a life that would last millions of years in bliss and pleasure, even if they were allowed to control everything in whatever way they wished, due to the inability of this worldly life to satisfy human desires and potential, they would continue to sigh and regret and wish for more. This dissatisfaction shows that humanity has an innate tendency to eternal life and has been created for eternity so that it can activate its unrestricted potential in an unrestricted realm.

A REMINDER

There is nothing without meaning or purpose in existence, and everything is based on a reality. This indicates the fact that in this restricted world, where pleasure is mixed with pain and many hindrances intervene; in this world which never lacks in envy and mutual wrongs, it is not possible for humanity to realize the perfections towards which it is innately directed. Therefore, there must be another, more spacious realm where nothing hinders another thing, so that humanity can order its worldly life along the way to perfection and contribute to the universal order so that it will earn eternal happiness in that spacious, eternal realm.

A REMINDER AND AN INDICATION

Although it is not the subject here, I have made an indication of the Resurrection. What I want to stress here is that the human innate potential is directed towards eternity. Consider the essence of humanity and the nature of its potential together with what is required to develop it. Then, visit the faculty of imagination which is the simplest and smallest servant of human essence. Ask, "O respected faculty of imagination! I have glad tidings for you. You will be given a million years of happy life in the world. You will be able to control everything in the world as you wish. But following this life, you will be sent to eternal non-existence without being returned to life." What do you think the answer will be? Will it receive your glad tidings happily or utter sighs and regrets? Be sure that the essence of humanity will wail in the depths of its conscience, and utter, "Alas! Woe to me that there is no eternal happiness!" It will reprimand the faculty of imagination and say to it: "Do not be content with this transient life!"

O brothers and sisters, look! If this transient happiness, even though it might last millions of years, cannot satisfy the faculty of imagination, which is just one of the servants of the human essence, how can it satisfy the human essence itself, which has many more servants, much greater and more important than the faculty of imagination? The only thing which will satisfy it is eternal happiness that lies in the Resurrection.

The third point worth mentioning in relation to the superiority of humanity over animals is the balance in the dispositions of the human, the fineness in its nature, and its tendency to make things better or more beautiful. Humanity has an inborn tendency to live in a way befitting its essential nature. It must not, and cannot, live like animals. It must lead a life befitting its essential honor. It is because of this inborn tendency that humanity needs to improve and decorate its dwelling place, clothes, and foods, and use sciences and crafts. It is not possible for an individual to have sufficient knowledge about all such sciences or crafts. Therefore, humans need to live together, co-operate with one another, and exchange their products among themselves. The satisfaction of this need requires justice and the existence of certain rules, as the desires, potentials, and faculties of humanity are not restricted from birth, and so can be the cause of aggression and injustice. Any individual mind or intellect is unable to establish the nature of this justice or these rules, as humanity is neither its own creator nor does it have true, all-embracing or universal knowledge about itself, its environment, and its future. So there must be a universal mind or intellect that has this knowledge. This is the Divinely revealed Religion. There must also be a power which can dominate the spirits and consciences of humans, and thus implement the required justice and rules. This power must have some sort of superiority over others. This power is the institution of Prophethood, which was founded by the Creator of the Universe Himself. It is He Who chose the Prophets and made them distinguished in many respects.

A Prophet inculcates the Creator's grandeur in the minds and spirits of human beings. The Divinely revealed Religion he communicates requires regular worship, which enables people to continuously and increasingly feel the Creator's grandeur. Worship directs thoughts and feelings to the Creator, which, in turn, lead to obedience to Him. Obedience to the Creator, Who is also the Supreme Author of the universal, magnificent order, secures the perfect public order in human life. This perfect public order is based on God's Wisdom. The essence of God's Wisdom is that nothing in the universe is purposeless and meaningless. The universal order, beauty, and harmony bear witness to this Wisdom.

If you have perceived the superiority of humanity over animals in respect to the three points discussed above, you have then understood that Prophethood is the central point of human existence, and that it is around this that human life revolves. Also, consider the following three points:

Firstly, individuals lack sufficient knowledge, accurate viewpoints, and the ability to know themselves in all aspects and dimensions of their existence, and they lack the ability to lead their lives in a proper way that will enable their happiness in both their individual and collective lives. In addition, they suffer whims, fancies, and errors, and are often defeated by their carnal impulses which require discipline. Therefore, humans desperately need a perfect guide and teacher; this guide is a Prophet.

Secondly, the laws and systems made by humans cannot satisfy the perennial needs and expectations of humanity, nor properly restrict its innate aggression, train its faculties appropriately, or correctly guide its potential and disposition to development or progress. This latter is inherent in the tendency of the whole of creation to achieve perfection. Human laws and systems are almost lifeless and do not last. Even though they are based on the accumulated knowledge and experiences of humanity over the course of history, they are unable to cause the seeds of potential in humanity to grow properly or to yield sound fruit. For this reason, humanity desperately needs a Divine Law, which will enable its happiness both spiritually and intellectually and physically, both in this world and the next. This Law must also guide humanity along the way to the attainment of human perfection through the realization of its potentials. It is the Prophets who brings us this living, life-endowing, everlasting Divine Law.

A POSSIBLE OBJECTION: We see that those who do not follow the Divine Religion may enjoy a healthy order.

THE ANSWER: If there is any order in their way, this is due to the affirmed or non-affirmed guidance and the effect of the Divine Religion and religious leaders. There has never been a community left completely devoid of the guidance of a Prophet, so even though many people reject the Divine guidance and Religion, they are not able to remain unaffected by the Religion. Any approvable, lasting order observed in any community has its basic source or roots in Divine guidance. With respect to other aspects that are incompatible with Divine guidance, the order of irreligious people or of those who do not follow the Divine Religion is bound to collapse, even though such an order may appear to have brought some sort of worldly happiness to certain people. In addition, a good order must be one which brings true, lasting happiness to an overwhelming majority of humanity. An order which brings only an apparent, transient, superficial happiness to a small minority in the world, while hurling others into subjection and humiliating misery, cannot be regarded as a good, approvable order.

Thirdly, any extremity in human behavior or moral standards destroys human potential, which, in turn, causes purposelessness and vanity. Purposelessness and vanity are absolutely contrary to the Divine universal wisdom, which is clearly observed to pursue purposes and benefits in everything in the universe, from the smallest to the greatest.

A False Supposition and a Reminder

On the pretext of giving priority to law and its observance, which have been brought to the attention of humanity after so many disasters and by stirring up public opinion continuously, heretical people suppose there is no need for the Divine Law and that it is possible to replace it with human-made laws. This is a totally false supposition. For the world has grown old and there is still nothing to prove such a supposition. On the contrary, although our old world sees the development of some beauty, new vices and evil appear in even worse and more deceptive forms. Just as the rules of wisdom are not independent of the rules of government, so too is the order of human life increasingly in need of the rules of the Divine Law and virtues that dominate human conscience. In addition, new systems of education and human behavior, which are regarded as having no need for Divine Law, are completely unable to train the three basic human faculties—intellect, desire, and anger—properly or to develop them into wisdom, chastity, and moderation or chivalry respectively, nor to sustain them as such. As a result, humanity is in desperate need of Prophethood equipped with the balance of Divine justice, which influences and penetrates human nature and conscience.

AN INDICATION

Thousands of Prophets who appeared among humanity proved their claim to Prophethood with thousands of miracles they worked. These miracles, which form an irrefutable proof and an absolutely true voice, announce and establish the mission and institution of Prophethood. They also function as a proof for the existence and Oneness of the Creator.

A REMINDER

Each science has its own principles and laws upon which it is based and each is founded on the orderliness of existence. But for that orderliness in existence, there would have been no laws or sciences. Secondly, certain pleasures and love are found in the basic purposes and benefits appointed for life, such as eating, drinking, and marriage. (For example, the basic purpose of marriage is reproduction, but the pleasures provided by love for one's spouse and love for one's children are the pleasures included in this purpose.) If we can see the Divine favor in this single fact of life, we can easily understand that there is nothing that is useless or extraneous in existence, and we can perceive that Prophethood, upon which the most fundamental purposes of existence or creation are centered, is indispensable for human life and existence. If there were no Prophethood, humanity would have come from a chaotic world and this world would have been thrown into complete chaos.

A REMINDER

O brothers and sisters! If Prophethood, which is the lesser of the two proofs for the existence of the Maker, namely the institution of Prophethood and the Prophethood of Muhammad, has been inscribed on the page of your minds, then we can proceed with the greater one, that is, the Prophethood of Muhammad, upon him be peace and blessings.

AN INDICATION AND A REMINDER

This greater proof is absolutely true. For, if you study the lives and works of the Prophets, all of whom have been recorded at the top of the list of the pride of humanity, and consider the meaning and mission of Prophethood, which is the basic common point among them, beyond the influences of the considerations developed over the course of time,[55] then you can easily understand the following reality:

The rights of the Creator and the created are the lights of Divine favor and munificence, and form the rays of abstract beauties in existence. All the Prophets, upon them be peace, adopted and strictly observed these as the basic principles in their actions. In addition, their treatment of their people, their people's view of them, their perfect altruism and selflessness, and many other factors all proved that they were Prophets. The attributes essential to Prophethood (truthfulness, intellect, trustworthiness, communication of the Divine Message, sinlessness, and freedom from physical and mental defects) were found in the most perfect form in Prophet Muhammad, upon him be peace and blessings, who appeared in the Arabian Peninsula at a time when humankind was at the threshold of its maturity, and became the unique source and teacher of all elevated sciences for humanity. This inevitably leads us to the conclusion that Prophet Muhammad was undoubtedly a Prophet. In addition to these proofs, all the proofs, including their miracles, which establish the Prophethood of all the preceding Prophets also prove Muhammad's Prophethood, upon him be peace and blessings.

Explaining Some of the Proofs of Muhammad's Prophethood

Introduction

Every act and state of Muhammad, upon him be peace and blessings, that is connected with his mission, proves his Prophethood. His absolute certainty in his actions, his indifference to objections—the fact that he paid no heed to the objections of his opponents—and his fearlessness clearly demonstrate his truthfulness and sincerity. In addition, he did whatever he did in accordance with the spirit of truth.

This great personage had absolute certainty in the truth of his mission, and so he paid no heed to the objections of his opponents, refused all offers of

---

[55] When we consider Prophethood and the Prophets from the window of the present versions of the Bible, we see how difficult it is to find a true notion of Prophethood in it, and how the characters of many Prophets are shadowed by groundless calumnies. (Trans.)

reconciliation and compromise, and showed no fear, hesitation, or worry in communicating his message, acting with an unshakable confidence even in the most perilous conditions. He always said and did exactly the right thing; he was always the first to practice whatever he communicated to others, and he established his message with his life. The seriousness, harmony, and consistency in all his sayings and deeds, and the perfect balance both in his life and his message are other irrefutable proofs of the truthfulness of his cause.

An Indication

Both his own time and the manifestations of his message throughout the succeeding centuries—the magnificent Islamic civilization, with all its aspects—have announced the Prophethood of Muhammad, upon him be peace and blessings, in a single, harmonious, and truthful language. In the following lines, we will try to present some aspects of this language.

There are four basic ways that lead us to understand and affirm the mission or office of Prophethood in general and the Prophethood of a Prophet in particular. There is another fifth one, but since it is known and has been written about much, it will only be referred to in this book.

The First Way

In order to know the sublime character or personality of the Prophet, upon him be peace and blessings, we should consider the following four points:

THE FIRST POINT: As expressed in the famous Arabic adage, "Having eyes dark from birth as if darkened with kohl is not the same as having eyes darkened with kohl," anything superficial or artificial cannot substitute for something genuine and original. Therefore, affectation cannot be lasting and persuasive, and one's nature or character reveals it in a very short time.

THE SECOND POINT: It is sincerity and dignity that connect character sublimity with the ground of truth. Like blood circulating in the veins, what maintains sincerity and gives order to all the dimensions of good character is just honesty and trustworthiness. When sincerity, honesty and trustworthiness are lost, the character "withers away."

THE THIRD POINT: Things compatible and consistent with one another attract and are attracted to one another, while repulsive and contradicting things do not like to be together. This is true for both the social and spiritual/ moral realms.

THE FOURTH POINT: A judgment that is given or valid for a whole may not be valid for each of its parts. (Although this is a generally true fact, Prophet Muhammad, upon him be peace and blessings, is an exception to it. That is, no act or state of Prophet Muhammad contradicts his Prophethood.)

Considering these four important general rules, we can look at the personality, conduct, and works of the Prophet, upon him be peace and blessings. As confirmed and admitted even by his enemies, the most admirable, praiseworthy qualities and virtues combined in this person and formed such a character that, in accordance with the rule that repulsive and contradicting elements do not like to be together, as the angels of heaven do not like to be together with the devils of the earth, so too the character of the Prophet formed of the most sublime qualities, such as honesty, trustworthiness, and honor, never stooped to lying or deceiving. Rather, he absolutely swerved away from such behavior. The spirit of this character, from which it derives its life, is absolute truthfulness; Prophet Muhammad always spoke and acted truly. Like an ever-shining light, this proves his Prophethood.

A REMINDER

O brothers and sisters! Do you not think that if a man is renowned only for his courage, he will not stoop easily to lying so as not to taint the honor his courage has gained him? So, how can one who combined all sublime qualities in his person stoop to lying?

AN INDICATION AND A REMINDER

We see today that the space between truth and falsehood is no greater than the space between two fingers. Both are sold in the same market. However, the space between truth and lies was not greater in any period of history than in the Age of Happiness, the age of the Prophet, upon him be peace and blessings. Truth displayed its beauty to the greatest degree in that age and caused Prophet Muhammad, upon him be peace and blessings, who had this characteristic to the greatest extent, to rise to the highest point of honor. Truth realized the greatest revolution of history through him and opened the space between it and lies and falsehood to be as great as the extent between the farthest east and the farthest west. It was the most precious thing and enjoyed the greatest demand. On the other hand, being something which reduces even the greatest enterprises to a corpse, lying was exhibited in all its ugliness and cast people like Musaylima the Liar to the lowest of the low. Being a poison, it lost its share in the market among the Muslims.

The Arab Muslims of that time, who were extremely careful of their honor, completely rejected the lie, which brought no profit, and pursued the truth as if in competition with one another. Other peoples had to admit their justice and the justice of the Prophet's Companions in the sense of truthfulness. It was because of this that the Prophet's Companions were regarded as truthful narrators of the Prophet's Traditions.

GUIDANCE AND AN INDICATION

History, including particularly the biographies of Prophet Muhammad, is unanimously in agreement that Prophet Muhammad, upon him be peace and blessings, whose life has been thoroughly recorded, and is known in the greatest detail available in history, did not tell the smallest lie before he was forty, the age when he was appointed as Prophet, and was known as Muhammad the Trustworthy. In addition, he never stooped to deception; he preserved his chastity to the utmost degree during his youth, when carnal desires are experienced to the most inflaming degree; he was always known to have, and accepted as having, the most sublime character; he was perfectly balanced in all his acts. There was nothing in history recorded about him that opposed these facts. When every person reaches forty years of age, they have formed an established character, which shows very few observable changes later. Therefore, one who does not admit that the great revolution which Prophet Muhammad realized after he was forty was based on absolute truth should blame themselves. For such a person must be nursing a Sophist in his or her mind. Even in the most perilous conditions, such as when he sheltered in the Cave of Thawr together with his closest friend, Abu Bakr, during the emigration to Madina, and when there was no visible sign of escape, the Prophet acted in the greatest confidence and feeling of security. This attitude of his alone shows his utmost certainty in his mission and his unshakable confidence in God, Who sent him as a Prophet; this alone is enough to prove his truthfulness in his claim of Prophethood.

The Second Way

When we enter the division of time known as the past, we should consider the following four points:

The first is that those who specialize in a branch of science and base their thesis on it will demonstrate eminence in that branch.

The second is this, O brothers and sisters! If you have some knowledge of human nature, you will accept that even a person who has little renown cannot lie to a group of people about an insignificant matter without giving themselves away through anxiety or unease. And yet there is a person who is unlettered, but has great renown and honor, who, while undertaking a tremendous task and needing protection against his enemies, easily speaks about great causes before large congregations (and the whole of history), and who, in the face of great obstinacy, acts without any anxiety or hesitation. Furthermore, no contradictions can be found in what such a person proclaims with such pure sincerity and great gravity. In addition, he does so in such an intense, elevated manner that it vexes his opponents. Will not all these show his truthfulness in the brightest sun?

The third point is that there are many kinds of knowledge which are only of theoretical meaning and value for Bedouins, while being commonly known in the civilized world. Therefore, in order to study and know the states of the Bedouins, you need to go to the desert in your mind. If you like, you can consult in this matter the Second Premise located in the first part of this book.

The fourth is that if an unlettered person expresses his view on the matters discussed among specialists or scholars, agreeing with them on the matters on which they agree, and explaining and establishing the truth on the matters on which they disagree, without having been contradicted later on, this shows his superiority and his being taught by an All-Knowledgeable One.

Based on these facts we say: It is as if, despite being unlettered, the Prophet, upon him be peace and blessings, had penetrated all the depths of the past with his ever-active, unrestricted spirit, had learned the states and secrets of the previous Prophets as if he had lived together with them all, and explained before the whole world all the basic principles on which all these states and secrets were based. He made these same principles the premises or primary foundations of his mission, clarifying them to their utmost points. In addition, the Prophet confirmed the truths to be found in the Scriptures that were sent to previous Messengers, and corrected the faults and falsehoods which had found a way into them over time. This shows his absolute truthfulness and Prophethood.

All the proofs for the Prophethood of the previous Prophets, upon them all be peace, are also proofs for the truthfulness and Prophethood of Muhammad, upon him be peace and blessings. Their miracles can be regarded as his miracles also. If you give some consideration to it, you will understand this.

AN INDICATION

O brothers and sisters! Sometimes an oath substitutes for the truth. So, listen:

> I swear by the One Who revealed to the Prophet the narratives in the Qur'an (the basic aspects of the histories of the previous Prophets and their peoples), and took his spirit into the depths of the past and to the peaks of the future, making secrets apparent to him, that the Prophet's most careful and penetrating view is free from being deceived and confused, and his mission is absolutely true, exalted above deceiving and confusing people.

The Third Way

We should consider the following four points and one conclusion that pertain to the Age of Happiness:

THE FIRST POINT: Consider that even a small habit can only be removed permanently from a small community by a powerful ruler and with great effort. Then, see how that person, upon him be peace and blessings, in such a short time removed numerous ingrained habits from greatly obsessed, extremely proud, and obstinate communities, using little outward power or effort, replacing them with exalted qualities that became inherent in their being, raising them to the rank of the most illustrious, renowned, exemplary community of history. So, if you do not confirm what a peerless individual this person must have been, I will have to record you among the sophists.

THE SECOND POINT: A state is an entity that has a collective persona the formation of which requires a long process. Triumphing over powerful, long-established states is not easy, and requires a long time and great strife. Devotion to such a state has become a second, ingrained nature in its citizens. Despite this fact, that person, upon him be peace and blessings, formed a well-organized community from small, scattered tribes which had been in continuous conflict with one another, and founded an extremely powerful, well-established state in so brief a time as twenty years. This seemingly small state triumphed over the two superpowers of the time with a single blow within ten years of its establishment, destroying one eternally, and defeating the other so decisively that it would not be able to recover until its collapse. If you cannot see the extraordinariness in this person's accomplishments, you will be recorded among the blind.

THE THIRD POINT: Force can only achieve a superficial supremacy. But conquering minds and hearts, being beloved of spirits, changing habits and natures, and establishing a permanent dominion over the consciences of people is something particular to truth, which nothing else can do. (The undeniable witness of the fact that such a person's victories are essentially those of the truth, of love, compassion, knowledge, and faith, is his increasing dominion over minds, hearts, spirits, and consciences, despite innumerable obstacles, and the fact that the Religion he has conveyed cannot be removed from either the minds, the hearts, or the lands it has entered.) If you do not know this fact, you are alien to truth.

THE FOURTH POINT: Propaganda can only produce a superficial effect and close the ways to reason. But penetrating the depths of the hearts, moving the most subtle feelings, developing potentials like a rose blooming, arousing hidden or dormant characteristics and causing the essential core of humanity to burst forth and blossom can only be achieved by the light of truth. Indeed, it was such an unequaled revolution that this person purified hearts so hardened that they were burying female children in the earth alive; he took such people and furnished them with the most sublime feelings such as love and compassion towards all creatures, including even ants. He realized this revolution, which was impossible to realize with the force of mere power or laws, in the Bedouin desert community. Everyone, with some degree of discretion, will confirm the extraordinariness of this accomplishment. If you have some discretion, you will also confirm it.

THE CONCLUSION: World history witnesses that one who is able to arouse and develop one or two feelings, characteristics, or potentials is considered to be a genius. For, if certain feelings, characteristics or potentials are not aroused or developed, any success realized will be unstable and transitory. So, it was only possible through the shining light of the sun of the truth that hundreds of feelings, characteristics, and potentials, such as freedom, devotion, love, self-sacrifice, and heroism, were roused, motivated, and developed in the Bedouin communities living in the vast deserts of the Arabian Peninsula of thirteen (now fourteen) centuries ago. I will thrust the Arabian Peninsula under the eyes of those who do not place this truth in their minds. Look at the Arabian Peninsula. After thirteen (now fourteen) centuries of scientific and technological development, send there (or even any part of the modern, civilized world) a hundred of the most renowned philosophers, pedagogues, psychologists, and sociologists. Let them strive there for a hundred years, and see whether they are able to accomplish one hundredth of what this person, upon him be peace and blessings, achieved within twenty-three years.

An Indication

Whoever wishes a lasting success must follow the way established by God, and know His way of acting. Otherwise, God's way of acting that manifests itself in "nature" will respond by causing any attempt to go to waste, and condemn those who oppose it to extinction in the deserts of nothingness. So, based on this fact, see and consider what subtle, genuine, and sensitive truths and realities there are on which the rules of the Shari'a are based and how impossible it is for human reason to discern these, and how sensitively the Shari'a preserves the balance among what exists in the existing laws of creation and the operation of the universe.

The Shari'a has preserved its genuineness and validity through so many centuries and revolutions, developments, and clashes in human history. This shows that the way of God's noble Messenger, upon him be peace and blessings, is based on eternal truths.

Considering all the points mentioned, listen with an attentive, reasoning mind: Despite being unlettered, having no material force, and never aiming at rulership or dominion, Prophet Muhammad, upon him be peace and blessings, acted in an unwavering manner even on the most perilous occasions; he conquered minds; he made himself deeply loved by hearts; he established dominion over consciences and natures; he uprooted numerous established bad habits and characteristics and ingrained in their place the most laudable virtues, moral excellence, and praiseworthy characteristics; he removed hardness from hearts and aroused the most exalted feelings; he developed the core of true humanity in his followers, and made them the greatest, most renowned exemplary community in human history; he founded a formidable state in as short a time as twenty years, which was later to become the greatest power in the world within another twenty years, and which was to remain so for almost twelve centuries. All these show to those who are not blind the truth of his claim, his Prophethood, and his devotion to the truth.

The Fourth Way

This is about the future page of time and particularly about the Shari'a.

You should not neglect the following four points in your considerations:

THE FIRST POINT: A person, no matter how intelligent, cannot be a specialist in more than two or three fields of science.

THE SECOND POINT: Two persons present a subject. One presents it on the most proper occasion with all its dimensions and in its relationships with other relevant subjects. This shows that person's expertise in this subject. The other one presents it superficially and in imitation of others. Even if you cannot discern the difference between the two presentations with your mind, your spirit feels it.

THE THIRD POINT: As explained in the First Premise in the first part of this book, if a discovery regarded as extraordinary a few centuries ago had remained hidden up until today, a child could have made it, as all the preliminary knowledge and conditions were already present. Taking this into consideration, go to the Arabian Peninsula of thirteen (now fourteen) centuries ago, and look around. You will see that an unlettered person deprived of any material help established a high standard of justice based on the laws of true knowledge, such as could only be as well worked out many centuries later as a result of many centuries of research, development, and discoveries; you will see that the Shari'a, comprising the principles of that justice, has the capacity to meet all the needs of the future until the Last Day. It contains such basic principles that it can expand and deal with all the questions that will arise through time. It declares that it issues from the Eternal Divine

Word and secures happiness in both worlds. If you are fair-minded enough, you will understand that the Shari'a cannot be the product of any human mind. It originates in the Divine Knowledge and was brought to humanity through a Messenger of God, who is Prophet Muhammad, upon him be peace and blessings.

THE FOURTH POINT: As pointed out in the Tenth Premise, the Shari'a guides every person according to their capacity of mind and heart. It is as follows:

The great majority of people cannot grasp abstract truths unless they are not presented to them in forms that are familiar to them. Therefore, in presenting abstract truths, comparisons, similes, metaphors, parables, or allegories are used. In addition, the great majority of people tend to accept as true what they perceive to be true with their five external senses. For this reason, since even preliminary truths and basic laws concerning physical sciences had not yet been established at the earliest period of its establishment, the Shari'a preferred to remain concise in these sciences in order not to confuse people. However, it did not refrain from hinting at certain basic truths concerning them.

A FALSE SUPPOSITION AND A REMINDER

Every act, word, and state of God's noble Messenger, upon him be peace and blessings, shows his truthfulness as clearly as the sunlight. But it is not necessary that every act or state of his should be extraordinary. The display of something extraordinary only serves the proof of a claim. For this reason, when there is no need for such a thing, a Prophet leads his normal life in accordance with God's laws that are applicable to everyday life. He must do so because he is a leader for his community in everyday life.

O brothers and sisters! The religious life, and the Shari'a that regulates it, both of which are necessarily in conformity with the essentials of the sciences and rational truths—necessarily so, because sciences are the tongues of God's universal book of creation, while the Shari'a is the assembly of His laws for religious life—encompass almost all the different fields of knowledge. To cite a few examples, moral training, purification of the soul, care of the body, management of the house, civil law, social order, general law, and so on. The Shari'a established detailed rules concerning some matters included in these and other fields of knowledge, while in others it promulgated general principles and left to human reason the deduction of necessary laws that were based on them. Specialists in all sciences and branches of knowledge, if unbiased and fair-minded, will certainly admit that the religious rules and regulations of Islam and the commandments of its Shari'a, which were given thirteen (now fourteen) centuries ago cannot be the product of a human being. Thomas Carlyle, one of the famous thinkers of the modern world, quotes from a wise German politician that after his research about Islam, he asked himself whether modern civilization could adapt itself to Islam and survive. That politician gave an affirmative answer to his question. Carlyle himself also acknowledges that when the truths of Islam appeared, like a brightly burning fire, they assimilated other systems of thought and religions, which resembled pieces of wood.[56] He is correct in his judgment because any fallacy cannot survive in the face of truth.

Despite a myriad of attacks from all fronts and endeavors to distort it, Islam preserves its truths. It can even be said that all those attacks and endeavors make the layer of dirt that has been placed over Islam thinner and thinner (as a love for the truth and a zeal for research develop in humanity). The present state of the world bears witness to this. The premises in the first part of this book should be taken into consideration.

A FALSE SUPPOSITION AND A REMINDER

If you claim that a person can have knowledge of certain basic principles and laws of all sciences, I will reply as follows:

You are right and you are wrong. In theory, this seems to be possible. But knowing something does not mean knowing it theoretically and superfi-

---

[56] Thomas Carlyle (1795–1881), a Scottish essayist and historian, gave a lecture on Prophet Muhammad in 1841, titled "The Hero as Prophet," and wrote his famous book, *On Heroes, Hero-Worship and the Heroic in History*. Karen Armstrong, a contemporary writer and historian of religion, evaluates Thomas Carlyle's lecture as the first attempt in Europe to see Muhammad as a genuinely religious man. (*Muhammad: A Biography of the Prophet*, San Francisco, 1993, p. 38.) However, many Western thinkers, partly freed from the prejudices of earlier centuries, have later admitted the genuine value of Islam and Prophet Muhammad, upon him be peace and blessings. See, Abu'l-Fazl Ezzati, *An Introduction to the History of the Spread of Islam*, London, News and Media Limited, 1978. (Trans.)

cially. There are certain principles and laws that must be known in all their aspects; these pertain to all times, conditions, and people, and they are different from one another. They are also of such a form that in them are reflected many laws and principles of other sciences. In addition, one must understand them with their practicability for the optimal degree of use in every condition and section of time. No one, however intelligent a genius they may be, can discover or establish these laws and principles. The same word can be uttered by two persons. But one may display his or her ignorance by doing so, while the other demonstrates knowledge.

AN INDICATION, GUIDANCE, AND A REMINDER

O brothers and sisters who have continued traveling together with me from the beginning of this book! Look with a broad view and reflect, and form a high council in your mind in order to reason properly. Then summon whichever of the twelve premises in the first part of this book you wish to consult. You can also consult the following principles:

A person cannot be a specialist in more than one or two or three sciences. The same word uttered by two persons may vary in purpose, meaning, content, and several other aspects. Sciences develop through studies and research; they support one another over the course of time. Something known today by everybody as a fact may have been only a theory in the past, and something known by civilized people may have been unknown to uncivilized ones. Comparing the past with the present and the future is misleading. The simplicity of desert people cannot tolerate the cunning and deceptiveness of the civilized person. Deception can conceal itself under the veil of civilization. Customs and events suggest and imply such things that they may cause many branches of knowledge to be formed. Human sight cannot encompass the future. The laws made by humanity do not last long; they have a "natural" lifespan. The environment formed of time and space has a great influence upon humans. Many things which were extraordinary in the past may be ordinary in the present, for the preliminary conditions and foundations for their comprehension may have long been prepared. Any intelligence, however sharp it is, cannot suffice for a branch of science to be formed and perfected, so how can it suffice for more than one science to be formed?

So, O brothers and sisters! Consult these principles, and then lay aside your soul which cannot submit to the truth easily. Take off the garb of whims, suppositions, false assertions, and groundless objections that the present time and conditions have caused your mind to don. Enter the apparently limitless ocean of time from the coast of the present, and land on the island of the Age of Happiness. The thing that will first attract your sight and attention is as follows:

A single person devoid of any help and formal authority confronts and addresses the whole world. He carries on his shoulders a truth heavier than the earth, and preaches an assembly of laws which guarantees the happiness of humanity in both worlds. That assembly of laws, which contains the essentials of all branches of both Divine and human knowledge, has the capacity to develop in parallel with the development of human capacity over the course of time, yielding fruit in both the world and the Hereafter. It establishes such a system of justice that it contains all the principles of setting up and preserving the balance in both personal characteristics and in human individual and collective life. If you ask the principles of that assembly of law (the Shari'a) where they come from and where they are heading for, they will answer, "We come from the Divine Eternal Speech, and accompany humanity on its way towards eternity in order to secure its happiness. Even when humanity's connection with this world will be cut off, we continue to accompany it. We will continue to guide and satisfy it in the realm of the other world."

A CONCLUSION

Doubt issues from three sources. If, being unaware of the purposes of the Owner of the Shari'a and not realizing that Divine guidance considers the different capacities of humanity, you deviate into a demagogy, which is a nest of misleading doubts and suppositions, your objections will arise from the following three points:

The first is that you may see the allegorical and ambiguous-seeming statements of the Qur'an as incompatible with its matchless eloquence that is based on its stylistic uniqueness, its clarity of statement, and its linguistic purity and fluency.

The second is that you may not be able to reconcile the Qur'an's conciseness and elusiveness in the "natural" facts studied by physical sciences with its guidance and methods of teaching and education.

The third is that you may not be able see some statements of the Qur'an as congruent with some rational and observable realities, and may regard it as unfitting for its purposes of guidance and establishment of truths.

O brothers and sisters! Help and success are from God. I say that these three points which you see as defects are not as you think. Rather, they are proofs of the Qur'an's being a miracle of eloquence. So, listen!

An explanation for the first objection: The overwhelming majority of people make up the general public. The Revealer of the Qur'an considers the level of the majority, without ever neglecting the academics or intellectuals. These latter can easily understand anything that is addressed to the general public, and so they will find their full share in the Qur'an's address. If the Revealer had considered the level of the elite, then the overwhelming majority of people would have been deprived of His Message. The general public cannot easily understand the abstract truths in their abstractness, so those truths should be conveyed to them in concrete forms. This requires the use of some literary devices, such as comparisons, similes, personifications, and metaphors, which we find contained in the allegorical statements of the Qur'an. The Qur'an has made them binoculars for the general public so that they can observe the abstract truths. Even though it is possible for some to be entangled in this usage and the apparent meanings of the verses containing them, and thus misunderstand some Divine truths—such as attributing a body, time, and space to the Divine Being, and comparing Him to the created—careful observation can easily penetrate the truths behind this usage. For example, when thinking on the verse, *The All-Merciful has established Himself on the Supreme Throne* (20: 5), a person can see the truth that God is the sole Ruler of the universe. The verse establishes in our minds God's supreme authority and dominion, and that God is not just the Creator of the universe, but also is its absolute Sovereign and Ruler. Having created the universe, He has not detached Himself from it, and has not become indifferent to His creation. On the contrary, He effectively rules the universe as a whole, as well as controlling every small part of it. All power and sovereignty rest with Him. Everything in the universe is fully in His grasp and is subservient to His

Will and Power. In order to establish this truth in our minds, the Qur'an speaks at the level of the general public and presents to their view a sovereign's rule of His country from His throne. This style of the Qur'an is described as "God's lowering His speech to the level of human understanding." You can also consult the Tenth Premise in the first part of this book.

Presenting abstract truths at a level at which human beings can understand with the use of literary devices is a requirement of eloquence.

An explanation for the second objection: This was elaborated upon in the Second Premise. Creation has a tendency to perfection, and humankind to progress. Sciences are the fruit of this tendency, and they have come into being via experiences and research, supporting and providing a basis for one another over the course of time. They have not come into being all of a sudden, nor are they independent of one another. Like both eccentric and concentric circles, they intersect and overlap, one within the other. The conclusions drawn are based on the foundations that were laid earlier. This means that a science which is still in the stage of formation will be a developed one in the future, and provide a basis for new developments and the birth of new sciences.

For this reason, supposing if someone had attempted to teach ten centuries ago a science or its established facts which have only recently been formed, they would not have escaped the commission of many errors or from leading their students into fallacies and confusion. If, for example, the students had been informed that it is the earth that revolves around the sun, not the other way round, and that there are more than one million living organisms in one drop of water, giving us a glimpse of the Creator's Grandeur, the majority would have denied their teacher and defied the truth. For they could not have perceived the existence of more than one million of living organisms in a drop of water, and would have had to suffer self-contradiction when their eyes were plainly seeing the earth stable and the sun moving. Confusing minds for many centuries would have been a grave error in and an obstacle to guiding people.

A REMINDER

Knowing something beforehand in no way requires that we base our present actions on that knowledge, neglecting what is happening in the present. For the sake of the guidance of future people, those who live in the present cannot be neglected. For this reason, both eloquence and guidance require that the truths that are manifest to the people in the present and the thought that serves as guidance should be mentioned with their clarity, but the truths unknown at the present and that will be brought to light in the future should either be ignored or, if we think we should mention them, mentioned in broad terms and allusively. Minds should also be prepared and kept ready for them, invited to investigate them. This is what the Qur'an does.

It is completely contrary to eloquence and guidance to throw minds into confusion by burdening them with what they cannot bear. "Speak to the people according to their mental capacities!" is a principle of wisdom. You can consult all the premises in the first part, including particularly the first one.

As for the third objection, which is not being able to see the apparent meanings of some Qur'anic statements as being in congruity with some rational or observable realities, after first consulting the First Premise, you should consider this: The four basic purposes of the Qur'an are establishing in the mind God's existence and Oneness, the Prophethood, the bodily Resurrection, and justice and worship. Therefore, the Qur'an refers to the facts of creation, which are the subject matter of physical sciences and can only be known through scientific study, parenthetically for the sake of its basic purposes. While mentioning the facts observable by everyone in every age clearly, it refers to others allusively and in broad terms, leaving their clarification to scientific studies over time and encouraging humankind to study them.

A REMINDER

It is a rule of both eloquence and guidance that the evidence should be clearer than the thesis and known prior to it. For this reason, the apparent meanings of some Qur'anic verses relate to the impressions sensed by the majority of people. However, these verses are not intended to provide evidence for those impressions. As well as serving for the establishment in the minds of people of the four basic purposes of the guidance of the Qur'an, they contain such subtle truths that they attract the attention of researchers and truth-seeking people. The verses of the Qur'an, clear in themselves and clearly showing the basic truths, interpret one another; some verses uncover the jewels of meanings contained in their siblings. Therefore, we should try to see those more important meanings that lie under their apparent, literal meanings.

A FALSE SUPPOSITION AND A REMINDER

If in order to draw attention to God's existence and Oneness the Qur'an clearly mentioned electricity, the law of gravity, the daily or annual movements of the earth, the formation of chemical compositions with the seventy (now more than a hundred) elements that have been discovered, and the sun's stability despite its apparent movement, then the proofs would have been more hidden and in need of explanation than the thesis itself. For this reason, the Qur'an uses a language that is comprehensible for every level of understanding and never throws its audience into confusion, taking into consideration the level of the majority of the people without ever neglecting the elite, and referring to certain subtle realities that will be discovered over time through metaphors, comparisons, and similes.

O brothers and sisters! The three points which some put forward to object to some Qur'anic statements are in fact miraculous aspects of the Qur'an and its styles. It is particular only to the Qur'an that it is able to address all levels of understanding and satisfy them at all times without the least contradiction or falsification.

> I swear by Him Who has imparted the miraculous Qur'an that the sight of the warner and the insight of the most careful one of humankind, upon him be peace and blessings, are absolutely exalted above being deceived or confusing the truth with falsehood or the reality with illusion; his way is pure and high above deceiving or leading to falsehood.

The Fifth Way

This is the way of the extraordinary states and experiences of God's Messenger, upon him be peace and blessings, and his miracles. The books of his biography and history are full of such occurrences. Renowned scholars have included them in their books and explained them.[57] Therefore, in order to avoid re-teaching what is already known, I will not go into detail about them here.

AN INDICATION

Not every one of these miracles has been narrated through reliable channels, but since there are many examples and varieties narrated through one, or more than one, reliable channel, all of them can be regarded as authentic.

One kind of such extraordinary experiences is seen in the events observed before and during the birth of the Messenger, upon him be peace and blessings, and before his declaration of Prophethood. It is as if that era had been blessed and favored with extraordinariness due to the noble Prophet, upon him be peace and blessings, and his advent was felt beforehand, and news of it was given through some extraordinary events.

Another kind is the correct information the Messenger gave about certain past events, and his numerous predictions concerning the near and distant future. It is as if his liberated spirit had escaped the restrictions of time and space, flying beyond the limits of the past and the future, seeing all time and space and giving us information about what had already happened and what will happen.

Another kind is the extraordinary wonders he worked in times of need, like a small amount of food being enough to satisfy many people, a miraculous increase in water, much like the above-mentioned increase in food, healing the sick and wounded with his breath, making some faces peerlessly beautiful and bright with a touch of his hand, and so on. There are hundreds of examples of this kind.

Another kind is the flowing of water from his blessed fingers. The abundant flowing of water—the basic component of life—from the fingers of his blessed hand, which was a source of generosity, brings to mind the effulgent flow from his tongue of the water of guidance, which brings life to spirits.

---

[57] Bediüzzaman Said Nursi discussed the miracles of Prophet Muhammad, upon him be peace and blessings, and mentioned about three hundred of them in "The 19th Letter" of *The Letters*. See, *The Letters* (trans.), The Light, New Jersey, 2007, pp. 117–236. (Trans.)

Another kind is trees, rocks, and animals speaking to him. It is as if the reviving quality of the guidance he brought had an effect on all things, animate or inanimate, and made them speak.

Another is the splitting of the moon by a gesture of his index finger. It is as if by splitting into two halves, the moon, which is in effect the heart of the sky, desired to have a connection with the Messenger's blessed heart, and split its own heart in ardent response to the gesture of his blessed finger.

A REMINDER

The splitting of the moon has been related through reliable channels of transmission and is mentioned in a Qur'anic verse as *The moon has split* (54: 1). Those who did not believe in the Qur'an were not able to deny this Qur'anic declaration, and except for a few insignificant, unaccepted comments, it has not been interpreted in any way that suggests denials of this miracle were made.

A FALSE SUPPOSITION AND A REMINDER

The splitting of the moon took place instantly at the time of sleep on a cloudy night, and at a time when the sky could not be observed as easily as today. It was shown to those who challenged the Prophet's Prophethood in Makka as a miracle, and therefore was not meant for other people. Also, as is known, the moon does not rise at the same time throughout the world. So, although there might be some who witnessed it in the neighboring parts of the world, it was primarily seen by those in whose presence this miracle was worked. Moreover, the Qur'an mentions it, and this has not been challenged.

A CONCLUSION

O brothers and sisters who are studying this book of mine! Please study the five ways discussed above in connection with the Prophethood of the noble Prophet, upon him be peace and blessings, with an awakened mind, a broad view, and balanced insight. Consider them as if they were a circular wall from which one could observe that illustrious person's Prophethood, or view them as if they were soldiers encircling the sovereign, and dismiss any doubt that may arise in your mind.

In conclusion, in answer to the question asked by some Japanese people, "What is the clear proof for the existence of the One to Whom you call us?", I say: Here is Prophet Muhammad, upon him be peace and blessings, as a clear proof!

AN INDICATION, GUIDANCE, AND A REMINDER

The science of wisdom sent a questioner and interrogator to the government of creation and came across the advance troops of humankind, heading for the future, and asked them, "O children of humanity! Where are you coming from? By whose command are you coming? What is your business here? What is your destination?" As the leader, guide, and spokesman of humankind, Prophet Muhammad, upon him be peace and blessings, gave the following answers to these questions:

> Dear questioner! We are all the communities of existence and have been sent from the royal office of the Eternal Sovereign by His command as obedient officials. The One Who has made us wear this richly embroidered dress of existence and equipped us with these capacities as the capital of happiness is the Eternal Ruler, Who is the Necessarily Existent Being, and has all Attributes of perfection. We, the communities of humankind, are here in order to be able to earn the capital of eternal happiness. We will depart from this world at a time and place unknown to us, and advance to the bodily Resurrection which is the realm of immortality.

O wisdom! Convey this to all without confusion exactly as you have been told!

The Third Purpose

This is about the bodily Resurrection. Creation without the bodily Resurrection would be meaningless. The Resurrection is a vital truth, and its clearest proof is Prophet Muhammad, upon him be peace and blessings.

Introduction

The Qur'an, clear in itself and showing the truth clearly, has clarified the matter of the bodily Resurrection to the extent that it has allowed no room for any doubt. I will try to mention only a few of the proofs the Qur'an has offered.

A SUMMATION OF THE MOST GENERAL PROOFS

The perfect universal order and wisdom in creation; the exact purposeful-ness of existence which allows no room for uselessness; the fact that there is no waste in the universal system and that all sciences point to the har-mony that is established in the uniform operation of the universe and on the basis of which they deduce universal laws; the constant repetition of daily, seasonal, and yearly instances of the resurrection of life in "nature"; the capacities and ambitions of humanity which worldly life is absolutely unable to satisfy; the limitless Mercy of the All-Wise Maker; the truthful tongue of God's Messenger, upon him be peace and blessings; and the manifest declarations of the Qur'an with miraculous exposition are all indisputable proofs of the bodily Resurrection.

EXPLANATIONS

1. But for eternal life, the magnificent orderliness of the universe would be totally insignificant and lose all its meaning, connections, and rela-tionships. The foundation of this orderliness is eternal life.

2. The eternal Divine Wisdom, which is the universal representation of the Divine eternal favor, has attached many purposes to creation. Without eternal life, all these purposes would be void, and as a result so too all the wisdom in existence.

3. As clearly demonstrated by observations and the life of the universe and confirmed by deductive reasoning, there is nothing meaningless or use-less in existence. This points to the fact that the eternal life will follow a bodily resurrection. To go into absolute non-existence would make all existence meaningless and useless.

4. There is no waste in creation. For example, the science of anatomy dem-onstrates that there is nothing useless or functionless in the human body. Likewise, the mental and spiritual capacities of humanity, as well as its almost unrestricted ambitions, thoughts, and tendencies have not been given to it in vain. This essential character of humanity demon-strates that it has been created for eternity.

5.   But for the eternal life, the capacities, ambitions, thoughts, and ten-
     dencies of humanity would be in vain. While the cover—the body—
     of that jewel that is worth the world is given infinite care and protect-
     ed against even a particle of dust alighting on it, how could the One
     Who has made the jewel break it up and destroy it eternally?
     Absolutely no! The care shown to the cover is due to the exceptional
     value of the jewel.

6.   All "natural" sciences originate in the magnificent, stable orderliness
     of the universe. The real purpose for the perfection and preservation
     of this orderliness is the eternal life that will follow the bodily
     Resurrection.

7.   Like the hour, minute, and second hands of the clock following each
     other to the completion of a day, the hour, month, and year hands of
     the clock of time follow one another; thus time progresses to a definite
     end. This self-evidently demonstrates that just as morning comes after
     night, and spring after winter, the night of the world will result in the
     morning of the eternal life of the hereafter.

     Each member of humanity is like a species of other existent beings.
     The light of thought has broadened its scope of ambitions to the
     extent that even if it swallowed all of time, it would not become full.
     The nature, value, viewpoints, perfectibility, pleasures, and pains of
     the members of other species are restricted, while those of humanity
     are constant, universal, and unrestricted. Daily, seasonal, and yearly
     cycles of a sort of death and resurrection can be observed in the lives
     of many other species, and these all point to the resurrection of each
     human and indeed of the whole of humanity.

8.   The capacities with which the essence of humanity has been endowed
     are sources of infinite abilities. From these abilities originate tenden-
     cies which give rise to limitless ideas and concepts. These ideas and
     concepts are directed essentially to the eternal happiness that will fol-
     low the bodily Resurrection.

9.   The Mercy of the All-Wise Maker, the All-Merciful and Compassionate,
     which gives a favor its true nature, and preserves it from being the
     cause of suffering, saving the universe from the laments that would
     otherwise arise from eternal separation, will confer eternal life on
     humanity. Were it not to confer this, the greatest of all Divine favors,

then all the favors coming in the world would become suffering and vengeance. This would mean the denial of Divine Mercy, the existence of which the whole of existence decisively proves.

O brothers and sisters! Think about love and compassion, which are only two among the infinite varieties of Divine favor. Then, consider eternal separation and the endless pangs that would arise from it! What great suffering love would turn into! This means that pangs of eternal separation cannot exist together with love. So, the eternal life, particularly the eternal life of happiness, will strike such a blow at eternal separation that it will cast it into eternal non-existence.

10. The truthful tongue of our Prophet, upon him be peace and blessings, the absolute truthfulness of which has been explained in the foregoing Five Ways, is a key to the eternal happiness that lies in the treasury of bodily Resurrection.

11. The Qur'an of miraculous exposition, which has been proven and confirmed for thirteen (now fourteen) centuries to be miraculous and inimitable in forty aspects, opens the doors of the bodily Resurrection and manifestly presents it to the views with all its contents and dimensions.

A Second Summation of Two Other General Proofs

This explains the two proofs of the Resurrection, which the Qur'an indicates.

In the Name of God, the All-Merciful, the All-Compassionate.[58]

---

[58] Bediüzzaman Said Nursi writes at the beginning of "The Ninth Ray" (included in *The Rays*), which he composed 30 years after this book:

It is a subtle Divine favor that at the end of *The Reasonings*, which I wrote as an introduction to the Qur'anic commentary, I wrote, "A Second Summation of Two Other General Proofs: This explains the two proofs of the Resurrection which the Qur'an indicates. *In the Name of God, the All-Merciful, the All-Compassionate*," and stopped. I was not able to continue. Thanks to my All-Compassionate Creator to the number of the signs and proofs of the bodily Resurrection, He favored me with writing the number of proofs of the Resurrection more elaborately.

Index

Index of God's Names and Attributes

ISBN 978-1-59784-129-0